STUDENT-OWNED LEARNING

STUDENT-OWNED LEARNING

It's more than the teaching;
it's about the learning

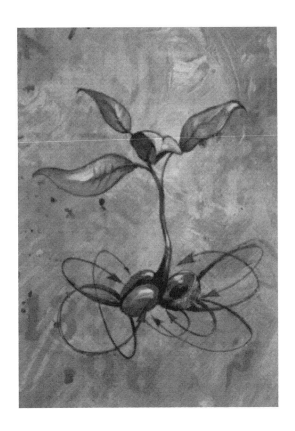

Debra J. Kennedy
Angela Smith

The Professional Learning Curve, LLC
prolearningcurve.com
North Canton, Ohio
2016

STUDENT-OWNED LEARNING
©2016 Debra J. Kennedy and Angela Smith

Published by The Professional Learning Curve, LLC, North Canton, Ohio

Cover design by Christopher J. Triner

ISBN: 978-0-9981199-0-8

CONTENTS

ACKNOWLEDGEMENTS

We are indebted to many individuals who have sustained us in writing this work. We have both worked with incredible educators in Ohio, particularly in the Green Local Schools, the New Philadelphia City Schools, and the North Canton City Schools. We are so appreciative of our cover designer, Chris Triner, whom we put on a strict deadline, and he never once complained. His art is fresh and inspiring, and we are excited that he could be a part of this work. The same kudos go to extraordinary English teacher, Julie Stolze, as she edited the book in just a few days. Additionally, we are grateful to expert educators and authors, Brian McNulty and Margaret Searle for their advice in publishing a book about education.

Our friends and family, whose names we sprinkled through these pages, are our support and inspiration. We are particularly indebted to our husbands, Mitchell and Jim, who have encouraged us in our educational journeys.

THOUGHTS ON USING THIS BOOK

"Good. Better. Best.
Never let it rest. 'Til
your good is better,
and your better is
best."
~St. Jerome

This book has been a labor of love for us, the authors, to share what we have applied and observed to be successful in the classroom. It is our hope that if you implement the practices within these pages that you will lead your students to be masters of their own learning.

This book is formatted for ease of use. Each chapter begins with a Theme-Explanation-Importance table. These tables contain the learning targets the readers should understand by the end of that chapter. On the sides of most of the pages, the reader will find quotations that have inspired us in our educational careers. We have placed them in gray, though, in case readers want to utilize the outside margins for note-taking. Additionally, each chapter contains reflection questions after the content so that the reader might consider the themes presented in those pages, and after the questions, are the references that the reader can explore further.

Lastly, our passion is to assist all teachers in any way we can. If you would like help with any topic, we are more than happy to assist. Please email us at prolearningcurve@gmail.com, and we promise to get back to you with some ideas.

We hope you enjoy and apply some of these practices . . . and if you do, your students will be the winners.

STUDENT-OWNED LEARNING
INTRODUCTION

Table I.1

Theme	Explanation	Importance
Student-owned learning	Teachers design lessons to engage students' needs and interests to accomplish deep acquisition of life skills.	The goal of all educators should be to develop life-long, independent learners.
Implementation dip	This decline sometimes occurs in confidence, outcomes, or scores when learning new concepts, skills or knowledge.	During this period of time when things do not go as expected, educators need to persevere to get through the dip; this is a key strategy for life.
Professional learning curve	The entire process of going into the implementation dip and then gaining knowledge from the newly implemented change is the real process of gaining new knowledge.	Life is about the challenges faced each day. The professional learning curve is about keeping one's eye on the vision.

OUR LEGACY

Kim was a student teacher whom the administration later hired because of her excellent performance. Her performance was superior because at her young age, she understood the demand of preparing lessons and the passion necessary for leading students. As Kim sat in the teacher workroom one day, busily preparing the day's work, a first-year teacher, Dan, sauntered over to her. He asked, "Why are you always working so hard? It's not like teaching is rocket science!"

> "We continue to be better today than we were yesterday because today is about tomorrow."
> ~Debra Kennedy and Angela Smith

> "Man's mind, stretched to a new idea, never goes back to its original dimensions."
> ~Oliver Wendell Holmes

This proclamation made it painfully clear: some teachers get it, and some do not. In fact, teaching is much more difficult than rocket science, mainly because it cannot be deduced to black and white mechanics. Skillful teaching that promotes student-owned learning encompasses so many nuances that it is amazing that it is done well at all. And, yet, teachers can discover and practice these nuances so that students truly change their behavior for the better by owning their learning--which is ultimately the goal of education.

Our story is a legacy to share with fellow educators: a combined journey of over sixty years of teaching, coaching, collaborating, and caring enough about the learning process to ensure that future teachers can start where we finished. Our motto is simple: "We continue to be better today than we were yesterday because today is about tomorrow." We desire to continue to invest in education by mentoring, modeling, and training others. The best legacy is not what we leave FOR people, but we what we leave IN people.

> "If you want the students to own the learning, then the teachers need to own the teaching."
> ~Debra J. Kennedy and Angela Smith

The fact that you have picked up this book indicates that you are on a journey to motivate yourself to regain your wonder and move out of an implementation dip to the student-owned classroom. We should all be in a state of continual improvement. Are you ready to start reflecting on your own needs and set into action a plan to move to student-owned learning?

Be aware, however, that growth, even the smallest of change, requires some amount of struggle. As you start adjusting one small part of your life, a storm of change will rain down on you. It is through this storm that you must choose the right path; this is the point when you will build your character. We call this the professional learning curve, and it is actually a great place to be since it is where the biggest learning is about to occur.

STUDENT-OWNED LEARNING AND THE IMPLEMENTION DIP

It is first important to understand student-owned learning, the implementation dip, and the phases that educators must travel along this path in order for change to occur.

Student-owned learning is a buzz-phrase in today's world of education. Why, then, is it so important? Think about the first big ticket item you bought yourself. Perhaps, it was a car. Remember how you treated your car. You washed once or more a week. You would not let anyone eat in it for fear of getting crumbs on the seats, and you drove it to an empty part of a parking lot so that no one would dent your door. Because you owned that car, it became your prized possession, and you were intrinsically motivated to keep it pristine. Now, transfer this analogy to learning. Think about the first time you ever completely understood something, and you were able to do something because of it. Possessing that learning is like owning the first item you saved for and purchased. Once it is yours, you want to protect and nurture it. If students truly own their learning, it becomes a part of them, and they will want to continue seeking further knowledge. Creating a student-owned classroom will drive pupils to a quest for more knowledge long after the teacher/facilitator is gone. And, this is the point of all education—developing lifelong learning. But, how does one create this atmosphere, and how does a teacher persevere when the going gets tough?

> "People do not care how much you know until they know how much you care."
> ~Theodore Roosevelt

Daniel H. Pink's book *Drive* (2009) proposes three elements to motivate people to change: autonomy, purpose, and mastery. Simon Sinek's book *Start With Why* (2009) suggests that people do not care about the "how" and the "what" until they understand the "why" behind any change.

We have seen change occur when all of these elements are combined with a sense of trust and collaboration. Unfortunately, when something changes, an implementation dip occurs. The implementation dip is the trouble that happens when something new is put into place before people are used to the change. It is at this point, that many people give up the new procedure and fall back into the old routine. Motivation to move through the implementation dip, however, must include:

"It takes courage to let go of the familiar and embrace the new."
~Alan Cohen

- the understanding of how the change affects the teacher;
- the change is not a waste of time; and
- the perseverance to push students to higher mastery.

Understanding that many elements drive change means realizing that stumbling blocks will pop up on the journey of learning. Again, some refer to this as the "learning pit" or the "implementation dip." But, to make it to the student-owned learning, and the "professional learning curve," teachers must assume the responsibility to learn and grow as an educator, even though sometimes, the implementation dip might be challenging.

A GAME OF BASEBALL AND THE CLASSROOM:
AN ANALOGY OF THE LEARNING PHASES

Contemplating the idea of change in learning abstractly can be somewhat difficult to imagine. To clarify the struggle that comes with change, consider a baseball game and its many phases.

Pre-Game Phase: During the initial play, teachers need teammates to keep them motivated and informed: administrators to place them in a scoring position while students and parents sit on their side of the bench for support. Any time teachers try something new in the classroom, building, or district, they must have access to the playbook, and it needs to be shared with everyone on the team in multiple ways. As Michael Fullan (2007) states in *The New Meaning of Educational Change*, initiation is the "process that leads up to and includes a decision to adopt or proceed with a change" (p. 73). This is the time for teamwork. For a team to move forward, a vision is promoted, and every team member ascribes to that vision. In a moment of challenge, educators must be able to revisit the "why" of what they are doing. It is the heart of any change and the force that creates the ultimate team for success.

The Curve Phase: "Play ball" is best used to describe this phase. This is where everything discussed in the pre-game is put into action. This can be a long phase, taking many years, and the seventh inning stretch can literally be seven years in the making. The players can see runs scored and plays happening, but the shift from pre-game talks to executing with precision may require extra innings.

"Life is like a baseball game. When you think a fastball is coming, you gotta be ready to hit the curve."
~Jaja Q

During this phase, teachers need to be supported continually by teammates: parents, students, and especially administrators. The implementation dip may occur here; this change may seem as if it has hurt the growth of the game, and if so, the initiative will die. Many educators will move onto something new because the new initiative proved difficult, providing no short-term gain.

In order to prevent a suspended game, the players will need to review the rules of the game and engage in additional practice.

- *Home Base:* How clear are the signals? Does everyone on the team understand the purpose? If a teacher is trying something new in the classroom, building, or district, is everyone totally clear on what it is and can express it to others?

- *First Base:* Is there action—has the batter made contact with the ball? Does every player have the drive to make it to first base?

- *Second Base:* Can everyone see how to advance to the next base? What are those next steps? Is there a clear pathway to get there?

- *Third Base:* Is there a coach nearby to help move to success? How do teachers get support? Is the purpose still clear? Is there anything that the teacher needs to do differently to continue home?

-

Post-Game Phase: This is when the routines become just part of the game. Even though the game is over, the practice still continues. When educators go through the entire process of change and no longer need to learn the plays, the change is ingrained into their culture of professionalism. Teachers just need to be careful that even

> "If you can dream it, you can do it. Remember this whole thing was started by a mouse."
> ~Walt Disney

> "Practice puts brains in your muscles."
> ~Sam Snead

though the game has ended, they will still need to keep an eye on their statistics to ensure to keep their averages at a high level.

Though we have compared the change process and the implementation dip in a sports analogy, note that more in-depth work is available in the research by various authors in the field of motivation and change, such as the previously mentioned work, *Drive* by Daniel Pink.

For our purposes, you need to reflect on any practice that you implement to determine the point of the professional learning curve and maintain the course. It is time to stop running from one initiative to another and become true experts by focusing on just a few great practices and engaging in them with integrity. This practice is guaranteed to lead to student ownership in the classroom. In the following chapters, you will encounter some familiar topics with the intention that you self-reflect on your learning process.

> "Even if you're on the right track, you'll get run over if you just sit there."
> ~Will Rogers

To keep your journey moving forward, you must identify challenges you are working to conquer. Always keep a vision for student-owned learning in front of you. Activities are not necessarily accomplishments. You must be willing to get out of your comfort zone and change. Unless you try something beyond what you already know and can do, growth will not occur.

CONCLUSION

Change is difficult, and many times people will not endure the process if they do not see immediate results. The challenge for teachers is to push through the difficult time period when they are not seeing results of their changes (the implementation dip).

If teachers use the science behind instruction, though, and have faith that their modifications work, then they will make it to the professional learning curve, where rigorous curriculum and high achievement abound in a student-owned classroom.

REFLECTION QUESTIONS

1. How many educational initiatives have you seen come and go in your career?

2. How do you want to be remembered when you retire?

3. When you have experienced an implementation dip, how have you reacted?

4. What strategies have you tried that are still effective in your lessons today?

5. How do you reflect on your educational practices?

REFERENCES

Fullan, M. (2007). *The new meaning of educational change.* New York, NY: Teachers College Press.
Pink, D. (2009). *Drive.* New York, NY: Riverhead Books.
Sinek, S. (2011). *Start with why: How great leaders inspire everyone to take action.* New York, NY: Portfolio/Penguin.

STUDENT-OWNED LEARNING
CHAPTER ONE
FINDING THE LEARNER WITHIN

Table 1.1

Theme	Explanation	Importance
Passion	Passion is the fuel for purpose in teaching.	Understanding the reason people do what they do is an important step in accomplishing their vision. A person's values keep his or her passion moving in a productive path. Values are made up of a person's core beliefs. Understanding how these three themes work together to form an educational vision is the cornerstone to creating amazing results.
Perseverance	Perseverance is pursuing a course of action even when it becomes difficult or discouraging.	In life, everybody faces numerous challenges, and in order to achieve any goal, people must understand that getting through the pitfalls and adversity requires a never-give-up attitude.
Motivation	Motivation is the factor that stimulates people to be interested or committed to take action.	Vision and goals are only plans. It takes action to bring them to life. If people have no intrinsic motivation, then they have no reason to do anything. Motivation drives everyone to complete a task.

FINDING YOUR PASSION

In the book, *The Passionate Teacher: A Practical Guide (2001)*, Robert Fried writes:

> to be a passionate teacher is to be someone in love with a field of knowledge, deeply stirred by issues and ideas that challenge our world, drawn to the dilemmas and potentials of the young people who come into class each day—or captivated by all of these. (p. 1)

"If you can't figure out your purpose, find out your passion. For your passion will lead you right into your purpose."
~T.D. Jakes

Fried divides teacher passion into three categories:

- passion for their field of knowledge;
- passion for the issues facing the world;
- passion for children.

On the path to discovering passion in teaching, you must reflect upon the meaning of the concept of teaching. Whenever educators discuss the art and science of teaching, the word art is placed as the first descriptor. Notice common descriptors utilizing the word "art" in their name: Arts and Crafts, Art and Culture, Art and Science, Art and Education. The significance of art preceding the other noun in each title is that art is a significant piece of the human spirit and must be cultivated through beliefs and values. Robert Marzano, in his work *The Art and Science of Teaching,* urges teachers to utilize research to identify effective teaching strategies, and to use that expertise to select the strategy that best matches the needs of the students. And, that is the art or spirit part of teaching.

"Change doesn't start with action; it starts with vision. Artists are great at creating visions."
~Steve Lambert

Understand yourself → Understand others

You must first understand yourself before you can help others to understand themselves. You must delve into your psyche to uncover your passion by examining your core beliefs. In school, students are taught about character traits such as trustworthiness, honesty, integrity, caring, respect, and responsibility, and these same concepts apply to adults. Until educators reflect upon these concepts and other beliefs that drive their thoughts and actions, it is difficult to understand what fuels the fire to ignite the passion in others.

To help you get started in discovering your passion and values, take a look at the list of concepts in Table 1.2 and think through each one of them. Circle all of the concepts that you value--not necessarily the ones you think should be your focus, but the ones that hit your heart. If a particular value is not listed that you hold close, feel free to add it to the list.

Table 1.2 ★ *Cards sort!*

respect

achievement	appreciation	Attitude
collaboration	compassion	Competency
creativity	dependability	developing people
ethics	family	Friendship
generosity	goal-oriented	Happiness
health	humor	Integrity
kindness	knowledge	Learning
love	optimism	Patience
productivity	resilience	Responsibility
serenity	spirituality	Success

Now, review the values that you circled, and narrow the list to the three to five values that truly trigger your actions. Now, to make this exercise more relevant, take the three to five values, and think about a time when those values drove you to act in a specific way. As you reflect on these situations, think about the effect that the value had when you acted in a particular manner.

> "Live your beliefs and you can turn the world around."
> ~Henry David Thoreau

This exercise is intended to provide insight into what captivates your desire to teach or the passion behind your actions. These three to five values or beliefs should be the focus of EVERY decision that you make. This is how you can build your character and stay true to your decisions and who you are as a person.

Once one finds the guiding traits of passion, the notion of how to keep going even when the going gets tough will reveal itself and lead to the building of skillful teaching. A true test of an educator's passion lies in the ability to connect students in the ideas and issues surrounding the content. If a teacher cannot engage a student with the content or make the content relevant to the student, the learning will soon be forgotten.

Review your values again, and ask yourself, do my values make me a role-model for learning? Acting as a role-model for learning is an educator's most prominent value to students. When teachers continue to learn and grow, they demonstrate what it means to be intellectually active. When educators fail to learn new material and strategies, they lose much of the ability to teach students to learn.

Passionate teachers show students what it is like to be a learner. The modeling of learning is the power behind the passion. An example of this type of passion exists in science teacher, Mr. Michael. The passion he possesses for nature comes to life as he takes his students on quests to search for salamanders. He demonstrates these searches during his class, and then he asks the students to collect and identify unknown types of salamanders in their own backyards. By following the lead of Mr. Michael's passion, students continue their scientific exploration after they have left the doors of their science class, and this learning truly becomes their own.

"Educators are the only people who lose sleep over other people's children."
~Nicholas Ferroni

RESPECT AND LEARNING

Another component of a teacher's passion manifests itself in the form of demonstrating respect for learning and modeling respect for others. The respect between teacher and student works the same way. The fear of being called upon and embarrassed in front of peers will prevent certain students from participating in class discussions. Many times, a failing grade for nonparticipation is more desirable than exposure to class ridicule. When students choose to withdraw from class participation, they are probably not learning the content. Teachers need to be cognizant of their values, beliefs, and attitudes to prevent the alienation of students if they want them to learn. Even micro-aggressions, such as sarcasm, can easily turn off a student's learning. So to be a model of learning, a teacher needs to concentrate on encouraging respect between and with students.

> "Without appreciation and respect for other people, true leadership becomes ineffective, if not impossible."
> ~George Foremen

TEACHING FOR THE GAME OF LIFE

One method to encourage classroom respect and participation has been researched for the past thirty years: cooperative learning, and the latest compilation of educational research by John Hattie discloses that collaboration is one of the top indicators for student achievement. In order for collaboration to occur, students must learn to work together as teammates, interdependently learning and adding value to their own process.

This development of mutual respect among classmates and the desire to learn challenging topics does not come in one lesson or even in one semester. If instructors are teaching for the sake of school instead of the game of life, they are wasting precious time. If students see

> "We are what we repeatedly do. Excellence then is not an act, but a habit."
> ~Aristotle

assignments of reading, writing, speaking, listening, and thinking tasks without real purposes, then teachers are just going through the motions of teaching. This type of rote teaching will disengage students from the real aspect of learning. This would be the same as being a baseball player and just looking forward to the ninth inning so he or she can finish the game without caring about winning or losing. Education is more than just playing a game. It is more than getting to the bottom of the ninth inning and finishing the game. Education is what empowers the next generation to become better than the previous one. Education is about the development of the human spirit. It is the call to be more than people can imagine being, developing their talents to make a difference in this lifetime.

In the book, *Teach Like a Pirate* (2012), Dave Burgess proposes two questions to teachers to determine if they truly have a passionate classroom.

1. If your students didn't have to be there, would you be teaching in an empty room?

2. Do you have any lessons you could sell tickets for? (pp. 58-59)

Some teachers fall into the rut of non-imaginative teaching because they feel handicapped by barriers, which really become excuses. The biggest excuses used to play the game of education are high-stakes tests, state-required curriculum, teacher evaluation systems, and most often used: the lack of time. Teachers need to contend with these issues, rather than treating them as barriers because the reality is for learning to occur, educators need to help students see that they are unique and valued as people. This can be accomplished by the teacher inviting the students into their lives through conversations about their family and interests outside of the school building.

Instructors need to move students from a spectator in the stands listening quietly to a presenter speaking to an actual player who will win the game. Allowing students to collaborate, voice opinions, argue, and assume choice in the learning process will propel them toward student-owned learning.

PASSION AND MOTIVATION

In the fascinating autobiography, *The Other Wes Moore: One Name, Two Fates,* two men with the same name both grew up in fatherless homes located in less-than-desirable neighborhoods in Baltimore. While the author, Wes Moore has lived a commendable life, the other Moore is serving a life-sentence for murder. To Wes Moore and readers, the question arises: what variables make the difference between a productive life and a life of crime? And, further, for our purposes, can a teacher truly make this difference in a student's life? We will address more on learning motives in the lesson in Chapter Two with essential questions to bring even the most reluctant learner into the ballfield, but for now, let us look at how you, the teacher can inspire the passion and motivation in the classroom. What are some of those practical steps to cultivating the student effort and performance that we desire?

Step 1: Have you discovered your personal passions? How about the passions within your own content? As you plan your lessons, you must place yourself in the perspective of a student. Decide what makes you eager to proceed with the content and build your lesson around the excitement. Your passion will excite the students. Even if they do not pursue a career in this content area, they can build appreciation for the subject through your eyes.

> "The results you achieve will be in direct proportion to the effort you apply."
> ~Denis Waitly

Step 2: We need to make learning "relevant," but what does that really mean? Think about it this way: If the students are completing an assignment for a grade, then it is only relevant for playing the game of school. Talk to the students and ask them what is really important to them; build lessons around the content that is interesting to them. If students can take pride in their work, then they will own and lead the work.

> "Create relevance, not awareness."
> ~Steve Jobs

Step 3: Society is changing at a rapid pace due to the increase of technological advances. Education is changing each year, but the difference between the rate of change in education versus the rate of change of society is leaving us with a large achievement gap.

Most curriculum is too extensive to cover well in one school year. If teachers spend time teaching at a level where the answers could be found in minutes with a cell phone on Google, then precious time is wasting away. As we take a deeper look into curriculum in Chapter Two, keep in mind that educators have to prioritize what is covered in a school year and plan units that go beyond recall and bring out the passion, consuming students to continue learning long after the teaching is over.

CHANGE TAKES TIME

If this all seems like a lot of effort and time, you are correct. The act of transformation or change does take time and practice. The best example that comes to mind is the metamorphosis of a butterfly. Most learn in their elementary years that a caterpillar goes through different stages while transforming into a butterfly. Caterpillars crawl around eating and living, never realizing that they must do something different. When the change process is invoked upon this creature, he goes through some specific stages, including the cocoon. If you have ever looked at pictures of the inside of a cocoon while it is being transformed; it is not a pretty sight. The messiness of change is something that teachers need to expect as they engage in new strategies of teaching. Some caterpillars go through the changes within a few days, while others settle in for the winter all snuggled in their cocoon. Just like caterpillars, educators may be able to adapt quickly and comfortably trying new things, and sometimes they may need a little more time to adjust. The important point is that a teacher has embraced the transformation process and is attempting to get better all of the time. The results of becoming a beautiful butterfly can happen again and again as a teacher stretches out and spreads his or her wings.

MOTIVATION AND PERSEVERANCE

Carol Dweck, famed Stanford psychologist, has been studying the factors that make people successful for most of her career. In her seminal work, *Mindset*, she defines success as stemming from having a "growth mindset." In his article, "Developing a Growth Mindset in Teachers and Staff," Keith Heggart, an Australian educator, summarizes Dweck's work eloquently:

> The crucial point for individual is that these mindsets have a large impact upon our understanding of success and failure. Fixed mindset people dread failure, feeling that it reflects badly upon themselves as individuals, while growth mindset people instead embrace failure as an opportunity to learn and improve their abilities. (para. 5)

"If there is no struggle, there is no progress."
~Frederick Douglass

Teachers want their students to have a sense of stick-to-it-iveness, but they must demonstrate and model tenacity themselves. In other words, if you try a new strategy, but finds that it does not work, you must polish that strategy and attempt it again—particularly, if the method is research-based and has proven to work.

"I am enough of a realist to understand that I can't reach every child, but I am more of an optimist to get up every morning and try."
~Preston Morgan

Obviously, teachers have a certain amount of grit—they made it through many hours of education themselves to get where they are; they, however, need to exhibit this resilience along with their passion in the classroom. This can be done simply by sharing stories of their struggles with students. Another idea is to explore the concept of metacognition—how does the teacher address his or her own lagging attention or disinterest in a must-do task? If you as an educator can consciously consider your own thinking, you can translate that exercise to students. Your growth mindset will be a model for your students to observe and follow.

Other ways to motivate students and you will be addressed later in this book, but for now, some critical ideas need addressing: first, teachers should review the importance of intrinsic and extrinsic motivation, and extending motivation further, it is critical to understand the concepts of short-term and long-term motivation.

Since much motivation research exists, most know that intrinsic motivation is the drive that comes from within a person, and extrinsic motivation is an incentive outside of a person. The longer lasting of the two is intrinsic, simply because it comes from the desire to do something. For example, Shay has the hobby of bird watching and wishes to see as many species in North America as she can. While many may find birdwatching to be the most humdrum of activities, this exercise is one that makes life more enjoyable for Shay. She reads about birds, investigates their habitats on the Internet, and every Saturday, she takes a day trip to places where she might catch a glimpse of a particular aviary species; in short, Shay just plain adores birdwatching. Will I go bird watching with Shay on a Saturday? No way, unless I can get Shay to stop at an ice cream stand at the end of the trip; in which case, I could be persuaded to go. Am I motivated to go birdwatching because I love it? No, my motivation is outside of myself—it is extrinsic—the reward of ice cream. Am I going to continue birdwatching with Shay if she keeps promising ice cream? Maybe, but probably not since I really do not enjoy the activity, only the ice cream, and how much ice cream can one person eat?

> "Insanity is doing the same thing over and over again while expecting a different result."
> ~Albert Einstein

Did you go into education because of an extrinsic reward of an administrative adulation and the enormous paycheck, or because of the intrinsic need to assist children with their learning? Most people enter the profession of teaching because they have the desire to make an impact on the future. This is not an immediate reward, and it is one that must be continually revisited to keep oneself pumped about his or her teaching career. Before teachers develop intrinsic motivation in students, they need to understand their own motivations about the education world. You have already discovered your passions, now let's think about your motivation.

> "Do it badly; do it slowly; do it fearfully; do it any way you have to, but do it."
>
> ~Steve Chandler

Answer the following questions honestly about motivation:

1. Do I give up easily if I find a task difficult?

2. Do I need a lot of variety in what I am doing to stay motivated?

3. Do I seek advice from several different individuals?

4. When I do not understand something, do I research it until I find the answer?

5. Will I complete a task for fear of being chastised if I don't?

6. Do I like to learn new skills?

7. Do I like to set goals and work to achieve them?

8. When I take classes, am I excited that I will get to learn something new?

9. Have I taken a professional workshop because my friend is taking it?

10. Have I taken an online class because I do not think it will be difficult?

From this inventory, you should be able to tell easily if you are intrinsically or extrinsically motivated. If you answered YES to questions 4, 6, 7, 8, you are mostly motivated by yourself. If you answered YES to questions 1, 2, 3, 5, 9, 10, you are mostly motivated in an extrinsic way. People are never truly motivated totally one way or the other, but to embrace a new task, intrinsic motivation is more indelible and leads to a growth mindset. If you find yourself teetering more on the extrinsic motivation path, you will want to revisit your passions and consider the actions that will allow you to blossom into a butterfly driven by internal motivation.

Now, that you have revisited your own motives and the importance of intrinsic motivation, how can you pass this onto your students? Many methods will be discussed in the upcoming chapters.

CONCLUSION

So to summarize: what do passion, perseverance, growth mindset, and motivation have to do with student-owned learning? Because the 21st Century has ushered in a sense of urgency and the demand for instant gratification, teachers often feel that if they employ a protocol in their classroom, and it does not work right away, then they should abandon it and try something different. But, if the teacher is employing research-based methods, then, he or she must cultivate those plans and provide them the opportunity to work—the teacher must have faith in the process to make it through the implementation dip to the student-owned classroom.

> "Don't give up just because you don't see immediate results. Know that each positive choice you make is affecting you in hidden ways—and will add up to big change over time."
> ~Karen Salmansohn

Now that you have more of a feel for your passion and motivation, you can rely on these qualities to pursue change with gusto!

REFLECTION QUESTIONS

1. If you had more than enough money to live the lifestyle that you desire, would you still be an educator?

2. How are you learning and growing each year? What was the last educational book that you read?

3. What are your passions outside of education, and do you ever connect those to the content of your lesson to build relationships with the students?

4. What lessons would you want your own children to sit through?

5. Do you wake each morning with excitement about how you can help that most difficult student?

6. When a student is struggling, do you want to send him or her to someone else for help, or do you want to research new ways to reach that student?

7. What kind of reflection do you engage in after teaching a concept?

8. What reasons have kept you from planning an engaging lesson?

REFERENCES

Burgess, D. (2012). *Teach like a pirate: Increase student engagement, boost your creativity, and transform your life as an educator*. San Diego, CA: Dave Burgess Consulting.

Dweck, C. S. (2006). *Mindset: The new psychology of success*. New York, NY: Random House.

Fried, R. (2001). *The passionate teacher: A practical guide.* Boston, MA: Beacon Press.

Hattie, J. (2009). *Visible learning: A synthesis of over 800 meta-analyses relating to achievement.* London, England: Routledge.

Heggart, K. (2015). Developing a growth mindset in teachers and staff. *Edutopia.* Retrieved from http://www.edutopia.org/discussion/developing-growth-mindset-teachers-and-staff

McEvoy, A. (2014). Abuse of power. *Teaching Tolerance*, 51-53. Retrieved from http://www.tolerance.org/sites/default/files/general/Abuse%20of%20Power.pdf

Moore, W. (2010). *The other Wes Moore: One name, two fates.* New York, NY: Spiegel and Grau.

Welch, L., Adams, G., Brown, J. L., Welch, A., Marzano, R. J., & Association for Supervision and Curriculum Development. (2008). *The Art and science of teaching*. Alexandria, VA: ASCD.

Table 2.1

Theme	Explanation	Importance
Curriculum	Curriculum refers to the knowledge, skills, and understandings that students are expected to learn. Curriculum includes learning standards, assignments, texts, assessments, materials, readings, instructional strategies and anything else to organize and teach a particular content.	Curriculum development is a continuous cycle of development, implementation, evaluation, and revision. Students and families need to see what is being provided to them for life opportunities. Teachers need to understand what is expected of them and contribute to the process. Educators should be confident that they are preparing their students for life outside of school.
Instruction	Instruction is the facilitation of another's learning.	Aligning instruction to standards through clear and concise strategies ensures a high level of learning. The unpacking of standards to guide instruction to accomplish the learning targets and to keep teaching on track and accountable to meet the specific needs of students.
Assessment	Assessment is the process of documenting a student's understanding as a way to gauge and improve teaching and learning.	In this chapter, feedback given during assessment is the focus of assessment. Feedback is an essential part of learning. Feedback through assessment provides student clear guidance on improving their learning.

C.I.A.: CURRICULUM, INSTRUCTION, ASSESSMENT

We conducted a recent professional development session entitled, Unmasking the C.I.A.; Debra's husband, Mitchell, an avid reader of the espionage genre, pondered the use of this title and thought that if we continued to use it, we might find our names on one of those

> "If we teach today's students as we taught yesterday's, we will rob them of tomorrow."
>
> ~John Dewey

government watch lists. We decided to clarify the acronym, C.I.A.: Curriculum, Instruction, and Assessment. These components work together to create a pathway for student-owned learning. **Curriculum** is the key that keeps the learning moving forward. **Instruction** allows for reading, writing, listening, and speaking to occur throughout the learning process. **Assessment** is an ongoing process to steer the course of thinking to deeper levels of student-owned learning. The journey through CIA can be achieved with teachers acting as designers who start with standards and travel the road of rigorous curriculum development. The implementation dip in this early phase of unit design occurs when teachers feel like the upfront work is not worth the end result of creating student ownership of the learning. As a designer of this unit, a teacher is an artist with a blank canvas, painting the best picture for learning to occur. If one designs curriculum in isolation, he or she encounters the possibility of getting stuck while brainstorming student-owned lessons. For this reason, we recommend collaborative unit design so that the team can encourage each other through the implementation dip and onto student-owned learning.

THINKING DEEPLY ABOUT CURRICULUM

The first steps in the curriculum design process involve analyzing the standards and thinking about the purpose of the content. We have found that as we work with teachers, however, the idea of unpacking standards begins to sound like someone pressing the repeat button from an earlier point in our careers. Furthermore, when we mention backward design, educators sometimes perceive this as stepping backward in time to use strategies we used to employ before the next best practice came along.

> "Optimist: Someone who figures that taking a step backward after taking a step forward is not a disaster, it's a cha-cha."
> ~Robert Brault

© Debra Kennedy and Angela Smith (2016), *Student-Owned Learning: It's more than the teaching; it's about the learning*

Ideas in teaching do cycle around in the world of education. A problem surfaces though when the educational concept looks the same but produces no better results. This chapter is a common sense way to transform that repeat button into an enduring passion button to ensure that unit design based on a solid understanding of curriculum is the key to unlock the balance between the art and science of teaching and to deliver student-owned learning. As Heidi Hayes Jacobs in her book, *Curriculum 21: Essential Education for a Changing World*, comments on Wiggins and McTighe's well-respected curriculum work:

> They are asking us to stop, reflect, and make intelligent choices, and to engage in backward design by beginning with the end in mind. They are asking us to be deliberate and forward thinking as well. Designing backward does not mean going backward. (p. 7)

"Designing backward does not mean going backward."
~Heidi Hayes Jacobs

Teachers find creating curriculum units that entice students to think deeply and connect to learning beyond the classroom to be difficult work. As we have guided teachers through the unit design process, we realize the necessity to give them the big picture first and then take it apart and rebuild the puzzle one piece at a time.

As mentioned in the introduction, Simon Sinek also makes this point in his book, *Start with the Why*. Table 2.2 provides the full puzzle to show the "why" behind each of the unit development stage. If the qualities of Curriculum, Instruction, Assessment are considered individually, then solidly woven together, teachers will design learning that students can fully embrace.

Table 2.2

Curriculum	Instruction	Assessment
Unpacking standards	Relevance to students	Formative
Graphic organizers	Motivational	Summative
Big ideas	Thought-provoking	Progress monitoring
Essential questions	Real world	Feedback
	Interdisciplinary	
	Collaborative	
	Performance tasks	

THE STEPS OF LESSON DESIGN

"You can't build a great building on a weak foundation."
~Gordon B. Hinckley

Prior to developing any unit, you must build a framework so that the unit can stand on a firm foundation. This process begins with a review of the standards and follows these steps:

1. Group the content standards into four to six piles in a manner in which they make sense to teach as a unit. This process can be accomplished in a variety of ways. Use index cards so they can be shuffled and moved so you can decide upon their significant parts. While completing this task, establish which standards are the priority standards. Priority standards are those on the state test blueprints and will be reassessed throughout the year to maintain mastery. Some standards may be touched on in other units: these standards are the supporting ones.

2. Name the four to six piles of index cards into units of study. Try to start with names that generalize the main collective learning from all of the standards in this unit. This will focus the work of unpacking the standards' meaning for students.

3. Prepare a pacing calendar or a YAG—year-at-a-glance chart. Using the names of the four to six units, put them in order and estimate how long to spend on each unit and in which months of the year they will be taught. No unit should span the entire school year. This calendar is flexible and can be adjusted as needed during the school year.

4. Collaborate with colleagues by considering all of the possible elements that could be included in this unit and how students will engage in these learning topics.

"Unity is strength . . . when there is teamwork and collaboration, wonderful things can be achieved."
~Mattie Stepanek

UNPACKING THE STANDARDS

With the completion of the above steps, the foundation is in place, and the district teachers will have a visual of where and when the standards will be covered. Next, teachers need to design each of the curricular units. To begin this process, you need to consider one of the most ignored parts of curriculum work: unpacking the standards. Most state standards do not clearly explicate what students should know and be able to do as a result of that standard. Unpacking, unwrapping, or deconstructing the standards, therefore, is a process that takes knowledge of the content and a sense of how to make that knowledge meaningful for the learner. This process is the key to developing aligned and relevant assessments.

KNOW, UNDERSTAND, DO = KUD

The first stage of unpacking is to develop a **KUD** for each standard. **KUD** stands for what students will **K**now, **U**nderstand, and **D**o as a result of this standard. This is the exact point where rigor is set. If the **KUD** is developed correctly, students will build their level of understanding and persist in the journey of leading their own learning.

Think of the standards as ingredients for a great recipe: they need to be measured exactly, or the taste will not be a culinary delight. Also, as you begin to teach, remember that isolated ingredients are not being served, and that each needs to be combined to serve a dish. This metaphor speaks to ensuring that the "**U**" in **KUD** is correct when teaching a particular standard.

The next several tables show an example of a group of eighth grade ELA standards pulled together to begin the process of developing a unit. With each standard from the unit, the **KUD** is unpacked. Examining each standard for the skill that the student needs to know is fairly easy since the verb helps indicates the skill of the standard. The other end of **KUD** is the "what" the students should be able to accomplish as a result of that standard. The most essential part of **KUD** is the middle **U** because it is the understanding students build by connecting that standard to their personal life. If you take the time to unpack this part of a standard correctly, students' motivation to learn will take care of itself. The understanding part cannot be written as educational jargon; you really have to reflect on how this standard could be turned into something that ignites energy into the spirit of the hardest-to-reach student in the class.

"Tell me and I forget; teach me and I may remember; involve me and I learn."
~Benjamin Franklin

SAMPLE UNIT

Name of Unit: Through My Eyes

Standard #1 (RI 8.3): Analyze how a text makes connections among and distinctions between individuals, ideas, or events (e.g., through comparisons, analogies, or categories).

Table 2.3

Know	Understand (My students will understand that . . .)	Do
Analyze and compare using analogies	People are alike or different from themselves	Find similarities and difference between individuals, ideas, or events

Standard #2 (RI 8.6): Determine an author's point of view or purpose in a text and analyze how the author acknowledges and responds to conflicting evidence or viewpoints.

Table 2.4

Know	Understand (My students will understand that . . .)	Do
Determine the author's feeling or purpose toward the subject...perspective	They can feel different ways about different topics	Discover the author's feelings toward the subject in the writing
Analyze the author's response toward conflicting evidence	They can argue against certain topics if they disagree by providing support	Find evidence to support the writer's conflict with the evidence

"Education is the key to unlock the golden door of freedom."
~George Washington Carver

Standard #3 W 8.3: Write narratives to develop real or imagined experiences or events using effective technique, relevant descriptive details, and well-structured event sequences.

a. Engage and orient the reader by establishing a context and point of view and introducing a narrator and/or characters; organize an event sequence that unfolds naturally and logically.

b. Use narrative techniques, such as dialogue, pacing, description, and reflection, to develop experiences, events, and/or characters.

c. Use a variety of transition words, phrases, and clauses to convey sequence, signal shifts from one timeframe or setting to another, and show the relationships among experiences and events.

d. Use precise words and phrases, relevant descriptive details, and sensory language to capture the action and convey experiences and events.

e. Provide a conclusion that follows from and reflects on the narrated experiences or events.

Table 2.5

Know	Understand (My students will understand that . . .)	Do
engage the reader	Their life story is interesting and can be shared	Write narrative
narrative techniques	Writing details can show their feelings about a subject	Use dialogue and description
transition words		Use a variety of transitions and other phrases to show sequencing
relevant and precise descriptions		Use sensory details and precise words to show actions and experiences
conclusion		Write a conclusion that summarizes the events

CREATING GRAPHIC ORGANIZERS

Robert Marzano has shown that one of the best strategies for learning is to create a graphic organizer. As you develop a unit, preparing a graphic organizer or organizational chart will be useful from the planning stages right up to the students taking charge of their own learning targets. In this chart, you simply separate the verbs from the nouns in each of the four to six unit standards to produce a visual that will allow you to determine the rigor of the unit. To measure rigor, you may use either Bloom's Taxonomy or Webb's Depth of Knowledge (DOK) or both. See Table 2.6. Dr. Leslie W. Grant's work, *Teacher-Made Assessments: How to Connect Curriculum, Instruction, and Student Learning* connects the idea of creating graphic organizer to align assessments.

"With organization comes empowerment."
~Lynda Peterson

Table 2.6

Standard	DOK 1	DOK 2	DOK 3	DOK 4	Remember	Understand	Apply	Analyze	Evaluate	Create
Analyze how a text makes connections among and distinctions between individuals, ideas, or events (e.g., through comparisons, analogies, or categories).			analyze					Analyze		
Determine an author's point of view or purpose in a text and **analyze** how the author acknowledges and responds to conflicting evidence or viewpoints.		determine	analyze				determine	Analyze		
Write narratives to develop real or imagined experiences or events using effective technique, relevant descriptive details, and well-structured event sequences.				write						write

[Handwritten margin notes: "Students own the learning, live the learning"]

[Handwritten margin notes: "6-8 units a year - 4-5 weeks per unit", "3 standards - unpack, name (title), big idea, essential?", "Connected Learning Channel"]

Another form of a graphic organizer can be a web organizer, a visual method to brainstorm ideas for your unit. This would be in addition to the aforementioned rigor chart; again, it is a prompt to visualize the rigor of the standards and to ensure that the lessons are at or above the intended level. This simplified graph, Table 2.7, helps the designer to think through ideas, connections, and more specific activities that the students might tackle during the unit.

Table 2.7

BIG IDEAS AND ESSENTIAL QUESTIONS

As mentioned previously, curriculum design is similar to putting a puzzle together, but rather than ending with the puzzle together as a stagnant picture, a teacher must continually examine the pieces of that puzzle, taking them apart and reassembling them, possibly in a new configuration. This cycle aids the teacher in understanding how the whole unit works. To reiterate the understanding piece of the **KUD**, the big idea of the learning is not something taught just for the sake of teaching. The big idea has to relate and connect directly to the student. This is one of the most difficult pieces to put into

"How you experience your present is completely shaped by what you believe your ultimate future to be."
~Timothy Keller

sentences because it cannot be written in educational jargon. This piece is critical if teachers want to excite their students about the content. As you read over some of the previous understandings from the eighth grade lesson, think how a thirteen-year-old student might react to learning about this concept.

SAMPLE UNIT: *What My Students Will Understand*

My students will understand that:

1. people are alike or different from themselves.
2. they can feel different ways about different topics
3. they can argue about different topics if they disagree by providing support.
4. their life story is interesting and can be shared.
5. writing details can show their interest about a subject.

These five understandings would lead to the big idea that everyone has a story to share, and in order to clearly tell that story, people must discover what made them what they are today. Imagine what might interest students in their early teens, or what their experiences have been. You, the teacher, need to walk in their shoes to draw out these experiences. For instance, students could have situations in their life that they are hiding due to pain of divorce, drugs, or abuse. They may not understand incidents that have shaped the way that they act or look, and you may need to lead them to these understandings.

> "Everyone has a story to share."
> Debra Kennedy and
> Angela Smith

If you can make the big ideas and understandings become the hook for learning, then you will capture the essence of motivation. Think back to when we first looked at the content standard of analyzing analogies. Would students get excited about that standard?

Does identifying analogies on a worksheet connect the learning to anything students are facing in their day-to-day life? Hopefully, you said, "no." Rather than having students complete hollow worksheets, a teacher can make learning seamless by connecting students personally to the content, eventually allowing them to lead their own learning.

> "I never learn anything talking. I only learn things when I ask questions."
> ~Lou Holtz

Another component of student-owned learning is through the essential questions introduced at the beginning of the unit and tying those to the big ideas. These questions are for the most part open-ended, providing students with conversation starters and allowing for deeper thinking about the subject. Generally, these questions spark the learning initially, and then, they can be referred to throughout the course of the unit. Ensuring that the essential questions and big ideas are wrapped around focused content is one of the keys to designing the unit.

SAMPLE UNIT: *Essential Questions and Big Ideas*

Essential Questions for the Unit Through My Eyes:

1. Why are there always different versions to a fight when everyone was watching at the same time?
2. You and your twin are separated at birth and raised in different parts of the world, and then you meet in middle school; how are you alike and different?
3. What is the best analogy that describes your life?

Big Idea for the Unit Through My Eyes:

We all have a story to share, and in order to tell my story clearly, I must find out what made me what I am today.

THE IMPORTANCE OF FEEDBACK AND ASSESSMENT

After the previous parts of a strong curriculum map are planned, it is now time to focus on the end or the assessment of the standard(s). To plan for effective lesson delivery, a teacher must understand the end target or the whole purpose of the unit. Please note that a distinction needs to be made between assessment and evaluation. Assessment is as an ongoing learning tool to guide the lesson delivery and understanding. Evaluation, on the other hand, should take place at the end of the learning, as this is the appropriate time to grade a student's learning.

> "Learners need endless feedback, more than they need endless teaching."
> ~Grant Wiggins

Grading students during the learning phase is not practical because it will not encourage students to lead their own learning by deeply exploring the subject. Feedback is the most critical tool to employ during the learning phase because it guides students to correct answers and deeper insights. Teachers should give feedback as progress checks after chunks of instruction have been presented and practiced with guided support. These progress checks are short and quick, e.g. holding up individual marker boards or short answer exit tickets.

Moreover, educators need to understand feedback fully by realizing that it comes in varying degrees. For example, praise, though it is a form of feedback, does not provide any direction for students to meet their goal. Carol Dweck discovered this point in her research and reveals it in *The Perils and Promises of Praise*:

> We found that praise for intelligence tended to put
> students in a fixed mind-set (intelligence is fixed, and you
> have it), whereas praise for effort tended to put them in a

growth mind-set (you're developing these skills because you're working hard). (para. 18)

This praise research indicates that teachers need to credit students' hard work, rather than using sayings such as "Kiss Your Brain," which implies that the students got the right answer only because of their intelligence.

Robust feedback that has actionable results for student achievement also has varying levels. John Hattie describes three types of feedback in his book, *Visible Learning for Teachers: Maximizing Impact on Learning*:

- Task   How well has the task been performed?
- Process   What are the strategies needed to perform
                the task; are there alternative strategies
                that can be used?
- Self-Regulation   Self-monitoring to achieve a goal

This research should compel educators to review the type of feedback they are giving students.

> "Students can hit any target that they know about and that stands still for them."
> ~Rick Stiggins

Some different forms of feedback can be seen in the examples in Table 2.8. After looking at the examples, try collecting some of your feedback that you give to students and see how much of each level that you are using during your lessons.

Table 2.8

Feedback	Type
Great Job, Barbara!	Praise
What do you put at the end of a sentence when you are asking a question?	Task
Last time you solved an equation, you solved for x. Look at this problem again and think about what we discussed last time.	Process
Do you think you met the criteria for an "A," Jim?	Self-Regulation

THE CULMINATING ASSESSMENT

As a final graded evaluation, the teacher must return to the graphic organizer in order to ensure appropriate rigor to meet the required standards. For each standard, the task must be designed around the level of DOK and/or Blooms. For example, in standard number one, the verb analyze is in DOK 3. The evaluation questions should be at least at this level of rigor.

Teachers can use the same graphic organizer to set up a blueprint for a test. See Table 2.9 to set up a twenty-five question test. Notice that a few questions are below the standard, while the majority at the required level of rigor.

"Learning is a treasure that will follow its owner everywhere."
~Chinese Proverb

Table 2.9

Standard	DOK 1	DOK 2	DOK 3	DOK 4
Analyze how a text makes connections among and distinctions between individuals, ideas, or events (e.g., through comparisons, analogies, or categories).		Q 1-2	Analyze Q. 3-5	
Determine an author's point of view or purpose in a text and analyze how the author acknowledges and responds to conflicting evidence or viewpoints.		Determine Q. 6-9	Analyze Q. 10-16	
Write narratives to develop real or imagined experiences or events using effective technique, relevant descriptive details, and well-structured event sequences.				Write Q.16-25

Designing the evaluation prior to planning the instruction guides the level of rigor and relevance in the day-to-day activities and will lead to student-owned learning. You, as the curriculum designer, must remember that if state blueprints exist for particular benchmark tests, then those should become part of the unit's rubrics. By including state requirements into units, you will never have to worry about how students will perform on high stakes tests because these are an inherent part of the everyday unit.

PLANNING ENGAGING LESSON DELIVERY

With completion of curriculum unit design, it is now time to focus on engaging the students through everyday lessons. In this phase of design, teachers must turn away from the everyday book, worksheets, and hum-drum lectures, and create experiences that compel students to attend class with curiosity and eagerness, the hallmark of student-owned learning. Since the standards have been comprehensively covered in the unit design, the teacher should be able to forget about the high-stakes tests at this point because they are a part of the unit.

"Allow creative problem-solving. In the real world there is no answer key."
~Nextlesson.org

© Debra Kennedy and Angela Smith (2016),
Student-Owned Learning: It's more than the teaching; it's about the learning

You now have the freedom to show your professional talents and provide the following qualities in a unit:

- Relevant lessons that connect to students' interests
- Fun and motivational activities that change frequently
- Thought-provoking discussions and simulations
- Real-world conversations
- Interdisciplinary activities (not fluffy thematic units) that connect information for students
- Collaborative work that requires reading, writing, speaking, listening, and thinking
- Performance-based tasks that include research, analysis, application, and self-assessment

> "Talent is always conscious of its own abundance, and does not object to sharing."
> ~Alexander Solzhenitsyn

A great resource to view this type of unit can be found at www.definedstem.com. On this website, you will see how scenarios are planned to hook students through real-life career video following the GRASPS model designed by Grant Wiggins and Jay McTighe.

Wiggins and McTighe note that authentic tasks include features represented by the acronym GRASPS:

- A real-world **G**OAL
- A meaningful **R**OLE for the student
- Authentic (or simulated) real world **A**UDIENCE
- A **S**ITUATION that involves real-world application
- Student-generated **P**RODUCT or **P**ERFORMANCE
- **ST**ANDARDS driven for rigor

Another concept to consider is that of Douglas Reeves's from his book, *Making Standards Work.* Reeves proposes the idea of taking mini-performance tasks and distributing them throughout a unit as a collection of assessments that masterfully culminates into a larger performance at the end of the unit. By chunking the assessment tasks throughout the unit, the teacher may use the incremental tasks leading to the main products/performances as a progress monitoring check or as grades. These mini-assessments should reflect the high quality standards, keeping rigor at its maximum level.

Teachers need to be cautioned here though. They need to check continually that the learning connects back to the unit standard(s). Occasionally, in an effort to make the learning exciting, teachers will plan an activity that while really fun, loses sight of student-owned learning and the intention of the big idea of the unit.

> "Helping students find a path to purpose is one of the noblest aspects of teaching."
> ~Vicki Zakrzewski

To design a unit around performance, you must rouse your inner teacher to be as innovative as possible. You should use resources and people to inspire new thoughts. Challenge yourself to design a performance task that the students will remember and own long after they leave your class. If each of these steps is followed in designing a unit, you will glide easily through the implementation dip because you and your students will find the learning exciting and enjoyable.

Since one size never fits all, the next chapter will look at the day-to-day instruction from different perspectives. Following John Hattie's research that unveils which factors increase student achievement, educators can employ the teaching strategies that yield higher results, assuring student-owned learning. Rightfully, instructors need to select the best teaching methods judiciously to ensure student ownership. Next, we will examine aspects of differentiation, direct instruction, and reciprocal teaching all intertwined with engaging instructional activities that you can take and use in your classroom tomorrow.

CONCLUSION

C.I.A.: Curriculum, Instruction, Assessment. Curriculum plays a critical role in organizing concepts to help bridge students' prior knowledge with future learning on the journey to student-owned learning. Instruction is purposefully constructed to engage and motivate students to lead their own learning. Assessments are designed to give feedback to direct the learning as well as how best to proceed with the lesson. The chapter explored the implications of aligning curriculum, instruction, and assessment. While each of these elements are explored separately; it is critical that they work together synergistically and need to be aligned in mutually supportive ways. Without proper alignment, student-owned learning will be difficult to achieve.

REFLECTION QUESTIONS

1. Think about your written curriculum. How can you begin to ensure that it is easily read, understood and implemented with confidence?

2. Which of your current lessons require students to read, write, listen, speak, and think, thus leading their own learning?

3. What has been your experience in reviewing the standards to determine if you are teaching them as they are intended and to incite student-owned learning?

4. How do you use assessment data to determine the next best step for your students?

5. How could you chart the type of feedback that you provide to your students or have students engaged in the type of feedback that they are receiving?

6. How can you collaboratively plan and talk to your colleagues about continually reviewing your curriculum for rigor and student engagement?

REFERENCES

Dweck, C. S. (2007). The perils and promises of praise. *Educational Leadership*, 65(2), 34-39. Retrieved from http://www.ascd.org/publications/educational-leadership/oct07/vol65/num02/The-Perils-and-Promises-of-Praise.aspx

Gareis, C., & Grant, L.W. (2007). *Teacher-made assessments: How to connect curriculum, instruction, and student learning.* New York, NY: Routledge.

Hattie, J. (2012). *Visible learning for teachers: Maximizing impact on learning.* London, England: Routledge.

Jacobs, H. H. (2009). *Curriculum 21: Essential education for a changing world.* Alexandria, VA: ASCD.

Reeves, D. (2013). *Making standards work.* Boston, MA: Houghton Mifflin Harcourt.

Sinek, S. (2011). *Start with why: How great leaders inspire everyone to take action.* New York, NY: Portfolio/Penguin.

Welch, L., Adams, G., Brown, J. L., Welch, A., Marzano, R. J., & Association for Supervision and Curriculum Development. (2008). *The Art and science of teaching.* Alexandria, VA: ASCD.

Wiggins, G., & McTighe, J. (2004). *Understanding by design professional development workbook.* Alexandria, VA: Association for Supervision and Curriculum Development.

Table 3.1

Theme	Explanation	Importance
Differentiation	Differentiation is a proactive philosophy that teachers use to vary their planning according to what students need to learn, how they learn it, and ways they can demonstrate it.	In education, the only way to be accomplished is for all students to be successful. As a consumer, we know that one size does not fit ALL; differentiation is about providing the necessary tools for students to experience success.

BECOMING A CHANGE AGENT

When we began writing this book, we realized that we could not just write about engaging practices for teachers to use in the classroom. The scope of our content had to include the reason educators must continually improve instructional practices; the purpose for each area of change; and the starting points that teachers could utilize immediately in their classroom.

Quite often, educators lament the changes expected of them—an issue that has gained steady momentum since the 1980s. In 1983, President Ronald Reagan's National Commission on Excellence in Education released the report, *A Nation At Risk: The Imperative for Educational Reform*. This report publicized the idea that education needed to change, and while the report highlighted important

"A high level of shared education is essential to a free, democratic society and to the fostering of a common culture, especially in a country that prides itself on pluralism and individual freedom."
~*A Nation at Risk*

---

deficiencies in education, it delivered no pragmatic guidelines to improve the inadequacies. For the most part, more than thirty years later, classrooms remain the same, with one teacher occupying 25% of the front of the classroom, and students sitting in seats to view the presentation of the content.

An even more daunting conversion in education occurred in 2010 when many teachers, parents, students, and community members were beleaguered by the implementation of Common Core State Standards (CCSS). Educational institutions experienced the implementation dip at this time because of the removal of local control over the curriculum. Prior to the CCSS, states determined the curriculum: they decided what students need to understand, and in many cases, little change in curriculum occurred. When states implemented the CCSS, student achievement plummeted for many schools, and educators were saddled with this implementation dip. To climb from this pit and put students back on the road to own their learning, districts realized that major changes to their curriculum would be necessary.

> "The capacity to learn is a gift; the ability to learn is a skill; the willingness to learn is a choice."
> ~Brian Herbert

Change, however, is hard work. As Willard R. Daggett discussed in his book, *Rigor, Relevance, and Relationships in Action*:

> The real issue is "Common Core was written in 2008 and field-tested in 2010. Think about the mobile phone you used in 2008 or even 2010. Common Core is already outdated! So yes, changes in education are coming fast, but not fast enough. Schools are changing, but the world is changing faster than we are--four or five times faster. We've talked about reform for the last 30 years, but little has changed.

We keep drawing lines in the sand and then stepping back because "'it's too hard'." (p. 13)

Yes, difficulty is a part of executing rigorous new initiatives; the vision of our work is that the change is worth the work and extra time to produce a student-owned classroom where all are motivated to learn. In almost every school, the mission statement reads something close to this: *Our vision is to prepare ALL students to become college and/or career ready, to become lifelong learners, and to become productive citizens.* Although this kind of statement sounds profound, the idea is not easy to accomplish in a classroom of thirty plus students from diverse backgrounds.

STUDENTS LEARN IN DIFFERENT WAYS

No two people are alike in every way, and environment plays an important role in the development of students. For example, the Kennedys are always hosting one or more of their six grandchildren. This variety of personalities demonstrates a picture of why teachers need to take a different approach to teaching. Anabel, the oldest grandchild, is dramatic and will learn anything as long as she is the center of attention. Trey does best with technology without a lot of interaction; while another grandchild, Henry needs to move constantly. Emma enjoys taking the opposite viewpoint and appears to be a budding lawyer, and currently, the youngest two, Ruby and Evan, are too small to indicate who they will be and how they will learn best. The point, though, is that each of these children learn and act differently.

"All students can learn, just not on the same day or in the same way."
~George Evans

As we think about these assorted children, how can teachers make school relevant for each one of them? If someone asks Henry to sit all day and listen to instruction, that is not going to move him to the highest rigor. If an individual requests Trey to turn off his electronic devices, his learning will be powered down. If Anabel is charged to work alone to complete an assignment, she will lose the collaborative learning potential that she seeks on a daily basis. So the question is: how does an instructor differentiate the instruction for a variety of students while keeping sanity as a teacher, especially to push the students to lead their own learning?

"The only way to get people to like working hard is to motivate them. Today, people must understand why they're working hard. Every individual in an organization is motivated by something different."
~Rick Pitinio

The journey of differentiation starts with a passion as discussed in Chapter One. What matters so much to you that you are willing to invest the hard work? We have answered this question by examining our motivation, which has been to assist teachers with their classroom curriculum when we worked full-time in school districts and has continued in our lives as consultants as we write this book. Both of us have a strong desire to expand our knowledge even after our departure from specific school districts. The future is dependent on generations after us, and we wish to impact them through their classroom teachers.

WHAT IS DIFFERENTIATION IN THE CLASSROOM?

In examining differentiation, it is critical to define it in terms of what it means to a classroom teacher. Many educators describe differentiation in an array of ways and execute it variously in the classroom. The leading differentiation expert, Carol Ann Tomlinson, has written books to demonstrate that this concept is a philosophy of how educators go about their daily work. In *Leading for Differentiation* by Carol Ann Tomlinson and Michael Murphy, the authors propose that students achieve best in classrooms where they embrace five steps interdependently:

1. Offer each student a positive, secure, challenging, and supportive learning **environment.**

2. Provide a meaning-rich **curriculum** that is designed to engage learners and built around clearly articulated learning goals known to both teacher and students.

3. Use consistent formative **assessment** to ensure that teacher and students are aware of the students' status relative to the specified learning goals, and that teacher and students both know what next steps are most likely to propel a given learner forward.

4. Plan **instruction** based on formative assessment information to attend to whole-class, small-group, and individual differences in readiness, interest, and approach to learning.

5. Work with students to create and implement **classroom management** routines that allow both predictability and flexibility. (pp. 1-2)

Since differentiation is a philosophy, educators must understand the theory behind each of these five essential components and what it could look like in the student-owned classroom.

"Teaching children is an accomplishment; getting children excited about learning is an achievement."
~Robert John Meehan

ENVIRONMENT

Providing a home-away-from-home environment is vital for students to feel safe enough to lead their learning. The physical space in the room should look inviting and attractive. Try this: examine your classroom to see what percentage of the room is considered teacher space, and then compare it to the space of the learner. This is a quick visual to understand who is important in the classroom. Decide if you are giving most of the space to students—the most significant people in the room. You can easily determine this by noting the amount of space dedicated to the students:

1. Are the chairs facing one another for collaboration or are they in neat rows facing the front to view the teacher?

2. Are there student examples of work hanging on the walls, or motivational posters?

3. Are supplies available for the students to complete their work efficiently, or are these items hidden away so that the students have to interrupt the lesson to ask for them?

4. Where is the teacher's desk located? Is it in the front of the room, set up as the "sage on the stage" and taking up about 20% of the total classroom?

"You can't make positive choices for the rest of your life without an environment that makes those choices easy, natural, and enjoyable."
~Deepak Chopra

 Also, examine the room for possible distractions, such as movement patterns to reach supplies or exit doors. When the desks are arranged for group work, are they easy to maneuver, or do you or the students find it difficult to walk around the room? Some features of a classroom that may be out of a teacher's immediate control are the temperature and lighting. To ensure students stay alert during class, a moderately cool room is preferable if you are able to control the thermostat. Also, plants enhance a classroom and provide better air quality. Organization is another key to creating a positive physical space. A critical part of functioning for learning is the ability to organize thoughts, projects, and materials, and a teacher must model this for the students. If the teacher allows a chaotic classroom, the students will observe the disarray and note that order is not relevant to their learning.

The emotional climate of a classroom centers upon the relationship between teacher and student as well as student-to-student. Students learn best when they feel safe, respected, supported, and connected to others. Sharing information with students is a great way to build this type of camaraderie *as long as the information is relevant to the students' situations or the current content of the lesson.* The bulk of the sharing should focus on the students contributing their story. Teachers must remember when sharing personal information not to discuss something that might cause anxiety. Students have their own issues that already consume their thoughts, and teachers should not add stress while building relationships. Each child comes with unique differences and needs to be treated with dignity and respect.

"Clean out a corner of your mind and creativity will instantly fill it."
~Dee Hock

Ideas to consider for building a positive classroom environment:

1. Keep the class interesting by tying assignments to personal connections.

2. Build humor in the classroom: bulletin board of cartoons; funny hat day; humorous books; laughing at yourself for a silly error.

3. Teach students the difference between being fair and being equal.

4. Point out success: send home positive postcards to parents, celebrating accomplishments.

5. Give students a voice: class constitution; class meetings; suggestion box.

6. Move around the room: try to connect personally with each student at least once a day.

7. Be supportive: provide activities that permit students to create and collaborate.

CURRICULUM

Chapter Two details the process of creating performance or project-based units. These curriculum units lead into differentiating learning for students based on their personal interests. Because every student is unique, a teacher must have a repertoire of protocols and include flexible grouping techniques to meet the needs of all of the students. This concept of tailoring instruction to the students' needs is quite different than marching everyone through the required text or curriculum in a lockstep manner. Since you are not teaching thirty clones sitting in the room, your instruction cannot be geared for the middle-of-the-road student.

"Education is the most powerful weapon we can use to change the world."
~Nelson Mandela

The concept of teaching-up is one way to ensure that lessons are tailored to all ability levels giving all student equitable access to rigorous, relevant, and engaging curriculum. This is different than separating students by their perceived current ability levels. When students of lower ability are grouped for intervention, the teacher is focusing on the skills and concepts, as opposed to assisting the high-achieving students who need to experience rich and challenging experiences. For the teacher, it may be easier to prepare and execute lessons based on this separation; yet for the students, it usually widens the achievement gap.

According to Tomlinson, teachers can differentiate three aspects of the curriculum—content, process, and products:

- **Content** refers to the skills and concepts of the curriculum. All students need to have access to these content at the same rigorous level. There should never be any watering down of this core content.

- *Process* refers to the activities in which students make sense of the content. These activities may be modified or tiered to accommodate the readiness level of the students or their interest level.

- *Products* refer to how the student demonstrates their learning of the content. This may be different depending on the student's interest or learning preferences. Some students may work individually, while others may prefer to work within small groups.

As stated in Chapter Two, curriculum is the map that drives students to their own learning. Through the curriculum design process, the lessons must continuously connect back to the learning standards to ensure a rigorous outcome. This is the difference between engaging curriculum and insubstantial curriculum. Insubstantial or "fluffy" curriculum appears to be fun and active, but little focus on clear outcomes exists, no research supports its credibility to work, and the learning does not remain in the student. With quality-designed curriculum, outcomes are always at the forefront, driving the process and products.

"The dream begins with a teacher who believes in you, who tugs and pushes and leads you to the next plateau, sometimes poking you with a sharp stick called truth."
~Dan Rather

Ideas to consider for providing a meaning-rich curriculum:

- Cooperative learning lessons
- Flexible grouping lessons
- Interest-based lessons
- Tiered lessons
- Multiple intelligence groupings
- Stations or centers
- Compacting

ASSESSMENT

As a doctor uses x-rays, bloodwork, and symptoms to diagnose and treat illnesses, teachers use assessments to diagnose learning issues in students. Assessment is used to determine the most effective strategies and activities to provide evidence of learning. Carol Ann Tomlinson and Tonya R. Moon write that many experts have delineated assessment for different purposes. Assessment can be divided into these areas: "assessment *for* instruction, assessment *of* instruction, and assessment *as* instruction" (Tomlinson & Moon, 2013, Location No. 530-539).

> "In an effective classroom, students should know not only what they are doing, they should also know why and how."
> ~Harry Wong

- *Assessment **for** instruction:* This type of assessment is often referred to as diagnostic or formative assessment. It is used to guide instruction based on how the students' learning is progressing. This type of a task is used with students in order to provide them with feedback to guide them through the new learning as well as guide the teacher onto next steps in the lesson.

- *Assessment **of** instruction:* These are known as summative assessments and used to evaluate the success of the learning. In most cases, these type of assessments are utilized to grade the students after their learning journey.

- *Assessment **as** instruction:* This process is sometimes referred to as student-owned learning and is also a formative assessment. These types of tasks are fashioned for the student to self-reflect on his or her own learning. Students set their own goals based on their strengths and weaknesses as demonstrated on these tasks. This task allows for metacognition because students begin thinking about their own manner of thinking.

Thinking back to the implementation dip and the introduction analogy of the baseball game, most students will follow this line during their learning journey. At the beginning of the game, assessment is diagnostic, determining background knowledge of the student and making connections to previous learning. This is the baseline data. As the lesson continues, and the learning becomes deeper, the ball travels down the curve where it sometimes get stuck or stalls out. *Assessment for instruction* comes into play with the teacher adjusting and scaffolding the learning to help students develop new connections in order to make it up the steep hill of learning. Along the way, as students begin to understand how they are climbing out of the implementation dip by thinking through the ways they learn best, they begin to experience *Assessment as instruction*. Finally, when students reach the top again and sprint into the home base, the teacher employs *Assessment of instruction* to determine their level of achievement in regards to the learning standard. Assessment ultimately is about the essence of the learning standard to show how deeply the student has achieved it.

> "Education is not the learning of facts, but the training of the mind to think."
> ~Albert Einstein

Some examples of formative assessment:

- Draw it: Ask students to draw what they understand or what is still unclear.
- Inside/Outside circle: Students face each other. Within each pair of facing students, students quiz each other with questions they have written. After a few questions, the outside circle moves to create new pairs. Repeat.

- <u>Four corners</u>:   Student self-evaluate and go to corner that matches their understanding.

  > Corner One: The Dirt Road (So much dust is blowing that I cannot see where I am going.)
  >
  > Corner Two: The Paved Road (The path is somewhat bumpy and old, and it contains potholes.)
  >
  > Corner Three: The State Route (The roadway is smooth going, but occasionally, I go too fast and need to slow down.)
  >
  > Corner Four: The Interstate (I'm traveling along fine and can even help others if they join me in the commuter lane.)

  Corners 1 & 3 work together and Corners 2 & 4 work together.

- <u>Cubing</u>: Small groups use a cube die to answer questions. Six questions are aligned to the numbers on the die. Student rolls and answers the question that corresponds. If a number is repeated, the student elaborates on the first response.

- <u>Circle, Triangle, Square</u>: Students identify something that is still going around in their heads (Circle); something pointed that stood out in their minds (Triangle), and something that squared or agreed with their thinking (Square).

- <u>One-word summary</u>: Students select or invent a word that best summarizes a topic.

A longer list, Differentiation from A-Z, can be found in the Appendix.

INSTRUCTION

After teachers have examined the curriculum and have a deeper understanding of the intended learning outcome, it is then time to put together a "game plan" to prompt student-owned learning. We have spent much professional development time giving teaching ideas for engagement strategies. In fact, we are dedicating an entire chapter to highly effective teaching strategies. During our own work, we have discovered that teachers love the sessions that add more ideas to their teaching tool belt; this type of professional development, however, sometimes becomes more of a checklist of multiple protocols to accomplish for teacher evaluation systems, rather than a rigorous, compelling system to increase student achievement. Certainly, nothing is wrong with trying new activities, but the idea behind differentiated instruction is for teachers to consider their classroom an action-research study that contemplates the current students' needs, skills, and interests. The first step is to utilize protocols to assist students in learning the content of the curriculum in a way that they may internalize and link the new information to their current knowledge. As the teacher connects the student and the learning through a new protocol, he or she should make adjustments until students are successful in terms of the assessment task. Along with all of this, the teacher needs to keep in mind the structure of the classroom or the environment created to conduct this type of learning. It is this cycle of learning that is at the crux of differentiated instruction. Differentiation is not a check-off list; it is a way of thinking and conducting the business of instruction.

> "If my mind can conceive it, and my heart can believe it, then I can achieve it."
> ~Muhammed Ali

> "Learning gives creativity; creativity leads to thinking; thinking provides knowledge; knowledge makes you great."
> ~Abduh Kalam

This process of differentiating instruction is what separates any well-intentioned teacher from a professional educator. Dynamic teachers do not just open books and tell students to read and learn or to jump on a computer and practice skills; they understand the background of their students and skillfully plan to have students assume the learning. Authentic learning—"of the sort that enables students to retain, apply, and transfer content—has to happen *in* students, not *to* them" (Tomlinson & Imbeau, 2010, p. 15).

Differentiation workshops often recommend this activity to clarify misconceptions about what differentiation is and what it is not. Consider Table 3.2.

Table 3.2

Differentiation is...	Differentiation is not...
Flexible groupings allowing students to work with students of varying strengths and interests	Labeling students by ability
Engaging tasks that vary by interest, readiness level, and preference around the same skill	Low level skills for some students and higher level skills for other students
Choices built around well-designed activities with common success criteria	Student free choice to do whatever they decide on any given day
Students learning to reflect on their own learning to make effective learning choices	Teachers taking on all responsibility for student learning
Classroom environment where routines, transitions, and procedures are in place	An unstructured and chaotic classroom environment

Ideas to consider for planning instruction:

- Differentiation activities that allow for individual preferences: i.e.: choice boards, learning centers
- Tiered or layered assignments that consider student needs and skills

- Differentiated formats, such as RAFT (roles, audience, format, topic)
- Anticipation guides that create discussion groups over topics
- Cubing: Rolling a die and completing the activity that corresponds (student interests)
- Learning contracts between the students and the teacher

More in Differentiation from A-Z in the Appendix.

CLASSROOM MANAGEMENT

Sometimes, teachers try a variety of protocols and activities in their classroom, but end up running from one side of the room to the other, exhausting their patience without gaining any different results for learning. Managing a classroom where students are completing multiple tasks and finishing at different times is challenging. Unfortunately, students do not come into a classroom understanding the dynamics of group work or how to manage their time wisely. In addition to planning differentiated activities, you must prepare students to work independently by transparently reviewing with them the curriculum, the assessments, and the instructional strategies. Here are some tips to continue on the journey through the differentiation continuum:

1. Communicate: Students and parents need to be informed and continually reminded of what you are trying to accomplish and how the shift is being made from a teacher- centered classroom to more of a student-owned classroom.

2. Take small steps: Teachers do not need to change everything that you do in one day. Start small and build on successes. Collaborate with colleagues to share strategies.

3. Prepare anchor activities: Expect that students will finish at different times so prepare options for students additional meaningful and connected activities for when they finish their main work. *A link for examples of anchor activities is in the *Differentiation from A-Z* in the Appendix.

4. Provide clarity in directions: When multiple directions are needed for varying activities, create index cards with the directions for students to refer to instead of insisting every student listen to each set of instructions.

5. Develop routines: As students enter the classroom, ensure that they have an assigned seat for quick attendance and any important announcements prior to getting to work. Keep this routine as well as a closing routing the same each day.

6. Practice procedures: Teach proper conduct for students to ask for help, leave the classroom, move the furniture, obtain supplies, and redirect their attention. These discussions about classroom conduct become part of the culture and should be sustained throughout the year.

7. Promote student responsibility: Help students become independent by putting them in charge of their learning. They can keep charts of their own tasks and self-monitor their learning goals.

> "Learning should never be a spectator sport where students watch the teacher do all of the work."
> ~Debra Kennedy and Angela Smith

Building a classroom around an aligned curriculum, instruction, and assessment, and incorporating sound classroom management techniques will connect students with their learning. Learning should never be a spectator sport where students watch the teacher do all of the work. Teachers need to "put them in the game" where learning is motivating and relevant to them.

© Debra Kennedy and Angela Smith (2016),
Student-Owned Learning: It's more than the teaching; it's about the learning

The classroom must become a place where students look forward to coming each day and are eager to discover the challenges awaiting them. Differentiation is making meaningful instructional decisions for the students so they will be compelled to invest in their own learning. This is the heart of student-owned, life-long learning. In the next chapter, we will add to your tool box by giving you research based strategies to make learning motivating for your students.

"Alone we can do so little; together we can do so much."
~Helen Keller

CONCLUSION

This chapter has placed much emphasis on the concept of differentiation. Differentiation, however, is really the basis to ensure that all students have access to worthwhile content that they can connect to life and will motivate them to lead their own learning. Hopefully, by considering and employing the aforementioned ideas about differentiation, you, the professional educator, will advance quickly through any implementation dip and find real success in the student-owned classroom.

REFLECTION QUESTIONS

1. Make a list of all of your students and see if you can name two personal things about each student. For example, Jim enjoys baseball and has a nine-month-old sister at home.

2. How do you ensure that your lowest student has the same access to content as your highest student?

3. How do you know when a student is not grasping the learning objective?

4. How do you decide the appropriate teaching strategy?

REFERENCES

Dagget, Willard R. (2015) *Rigor, relevance, and relationships in action—innovative leadership and best practices for school improvement.* Rexford, NY: International Center for Leadership in Education.

Tomlinson, C. A., & Imbeau, M. B. (2010). *Leading and managing a differentiated classroom.* Alexandria, VA: ASCD.

Tomlinson, C. A., & Moon, T. R. (2013). *Assessment and student success in a differentiated classroom.* Alexandria, VA: ASCD.

Tomlinson, C. A., & Murphy, M. (2015). *Leading for differentiation: Growing teachers who grow kids.* Alexandria, VA: ASCD.

United States. National Commission on Excellence in Education. (1983). *A nation at risk: The imperative for educational reform: A report to the nation and the Secretary of Education, United States Department of Education.* Washington, D.C.: The Commission.

Table 4.1

Theme	Explanation	Importance
Metacognition	Metacognition is thinking about one's own thinking. It is monitoring how a person learns, by reflecting on such processes as study skills, memory capabilities, and the ability to self-regulate thoughts.	Metacognition is the foundation for: • Independent reading • Independent writing • Independent thinking
Direct Instruction Strategy	Direct Instruction is a teaching strategy that focuses on curriculum design combined with effective instructional delivery and interactions between teacher and student. This approach is mostly teacher-driven.	These well-sequenced lessons produce high student achievement in both basic skills and problem solving in addition to increasing scores.
Reciprocal Teaching Strategy	Reciprocal teaching is a strategy where teacher and student share the role of leading the discussion using the four key elements: predicting, questioning, summarizing, and clarifying. This strategy is mostly student-driven.	This technique helps students to discern important ideas and have meaningful conversations.

STRATEGY VERSUS PROTOCOL

The aim of this chapter is to highlight the two effective strategies that research shows impact student learning. A point of clarification needs to be made here: when we use the word **strategy** to discuss lessons, it is the overall system used for the lesson, such as Direct Instruction or Reciprocal Teaching. The activities utilized within the lesson that engage the students are the **protocols** that comprise that strategy. In other words, strategies and protocols are not interchangeable. If a teacher uses think-pair-share, for example, he or she is employing a **protocol** for active learning. If a teacher decides to plan a lesson around Direct Instruction, then he or she is using a **strategy** for that the broader lesson within a unit.

This section will provide the requirements of each **strategy** with **protocols** to engage students and lead them to own their learning. While these protocols/techniques are important to a teacher's toolbox, your learning will increase significantly when you reflect on the change in your instruction when utilizing the strategy. As Dr. John Hattie explains in his book, *Visible Learning for Teachers: Maximizing Impact on Learning*:

> Visible teaching and learning occur when there is deliberate practice aimed at attaining mastery of the goal, when there is feedback given and sought, and when there are active passionate, and engaging people (teacher, students, peers) participating in the act of learning. It is teachers seeing learning through the eyes of students, and students seeing teaching as the key to their ongoing learning. The remarkable feature of the evidence is that the greatest effects on student learning occur when teachers become learners of their own teaching and when students become their own teachers. (p. 18)

METACOGNITION

The animated Disney movie, *Inside Out*, takes the viewer on a journey inside a girl's mind to discover characters portraying her emotions, and the plot centers on how the girl needs those different emotions to stay healthy and happy. Imagine a similar movie focused on the cognitive functions that happen during the journey of new learning. Because the acquisition of knowledge occurs inside the mind of a student, it cannot be seen, but if the learning processes are conceived as characters, the learning journey is easier to visualize.

First, envision a character inside a student's head called *Force*. *Force* represents the tension experienced from not knowing the content about to be taught. *Force* reacts by running around looking for ways to connect the old knowledge to this new knowledge. *Force* is necessary to create that need-to-know attitude or commitment to the learning.

Another character in the cognitive journey is *Center*, as in centering oneself by concentrating. As *Center* sits inside the brain, he needs total attention on the learning at hand so he keeps his eyes focused on the new information being sent in through all of the senses. Now, consider *Spy*; he is dressed in black leotards, jumping around the brain continually scrutinizing all of the new information and furtively considering how to execute the next activity. Also, do not forget *Artist* who organizes all of the skills necessary to sculpt a new learning masterpiece for the brain.

Working with the team, *Artist* builds a memory vessel that sends the information to islands in the brain, called Social Studies, English, Mathematics, Science, and any other subject that the student may be examining at the time. The bridges between the islands in the brain are maintained by another character, *Stretch* who allows information from one island to travel back and forth so interdisciplinary associations occur and are used when the student functions outside of the classroom. As long as this team collaborates and understands

"Whether you think you can, or you think you can't— you're right."
~Henry David Thoreau

the implication of their roles, learning occurs and is sustained long-term in the student's mind.

Teachers should continually provide students with new learning protocols, as these will assist students with organizing and connecting the processes happening inside their minds. Using active learning techniques allow students to practice the tension of new material (Force), focus on important details (Center), practice new learning (Spy), gather the necessary background skills to connect the new learning with previous knowledge (Artist), and utilize the newly gained knowledge to apply to everyday life (Stretch). As teachers lead students to understand how they learn, they are providing them with the powerful tool of metacognition; by practicing metacognition, students can become self-regulators who own their learning.

THE ACT OF LEARNING

Educators must examine the teaching separately from the learning to understand how these concepts work together. As discussed earlier, teaching is both an art and a science. Learning also has two components: linking and thinking. One of the best ways to ensure "linking and thinking" is to use the idea of *Backward Design* promoted by Grant Wiggins and Jay McTighe. Understanding success criteria—the benchmarks that help teachers decide if students have met the learning intention—when deciding upon a strategy or protocol, will allow teachers to activate all of the "characters" required for a student to learn. Moreover, teaching students metacognition and helping them to articulate where they are in their learning process will carry them from their prior knowledge to the advanced knowledge.

"We now accept the fact that learning is a lifelong process of keeping abreast of change. And the most pressing task is to teach people how to learn."
~PeterF. Drucker

When selecting an instructional practice, a teacher must prioritize by selecting the protocol that supports students in attaining the success criteria. Though many active learning protocols are fun and create an atmosphere of camaraderie, students need to understand that learning can be difficult work as well. Many educational publications center on different methods or protocols; you, however, should learn a few protocols deeply and develop the automaticity to implement the best approach into particular lessons—just as you want the students to develop automaticity with the material they are learning.

Think about knowing a process so well that it becomes a part of your being—this is what every educator should want for themselves and their students. For example, Angela has been golfing for many years now, but when she first began, she realized that the mechanics of the swing were something to which she would need to devote ongoing study, by practicing repeatedly so that the action of hitting a small ball with a long club would become an automatic movement. This comprehensive investigation involved the following course of action: Angela likes to analyze new learning closely so the first thing she did was to read several books and view several videos about golf. Next, she took lessons from a golf professional to develop proper form and muscle memory. Since the beginning of this journey, Angela has practiced the golf swing by going to the driving range, swinging the same club, hitting many balls, and analyzing the ball flight so that she can determine the best method to execute an excellent game of golf. The repetition of practice and the continual feedback has improved Angela's golf game, and this same situation can be applied to the act of teaching students techniques for learning.

> "In all planning, you make a list and you set priorities."
> ~Alan Lakein

> "The ultimate goal
> of all teachers
> should be to have
> their students lead
> and own their
> learning."
> ~Debra Kennedy and
> Angela Smith

The ultimate goal of all teachers should be to have their students lead and own their learning; the key to student-owned learning is to provide an environment with approaches that permit students to monitor, practice, and execute their own learning. This requires teachers to create classrooms where students have some control by providing choices in resources and assignments, and by allowing students the opportunity to make mistakes without affecting their report card grade. This environment also requires the teaching to be specific to the learning intentions and success criteria. When teachers design instruction around an effective strategy and then monitor the learning to determine if that strategy worked, student achievement is at its maximum.

This chapter includes two effective, researched-based learning strategies: Direct Instruction (a teacher-driven approach) and Reciprocal Teaching (a student-driven approach). Each strategy includes our ideas for protocols to employ when using that particular method. Although several protocols are listed here, teachers must remember to continue to develop more protocols each year to add to their repertoire. Struggling students are in most need of a variety of useful learning techniques when they find themselves stuck in their acquisition of knowledge or skill. Teachers must supply students with a myriad of ways to engage, collaborate, and self-regulate their learning.

DIRECT INSTRUCTION

In visiting thousands of classrooms and working daily with classroom teachers, our most surprising find is the discrepancy in definitions of what direct instruction looks and sounds like in the classroom. Answers include teacher lecture, learning objectives, modeling, gradual release of responsibility, guided practice, and formative assessment. What is even more interesting is the wide range of implementation of these sundry methodologies. Since the 1970s, educational researchers have tendered diverse approaches in designing a direct instruction lesson: i.e., Robert Gagne's *Nine Events of Instruction*; Madeline Hunter's *Seven Step Lesson Plan Model*; John Hollingsworth and Silvia Ybarra's *Ten Steps of Explicit Direct Instruction*. Although the stages are defined differently, all of these models hold the common viewpoint that the teacher is the focus of the process of instruction—which does not always lead to student control or student-owned learning.

> "Practice is the hardest part of learning, and training is the essence of transformation."
> ~Ann Voskamp

For the purposes here, we will emphasize a six-stage model of instruction that acknowledges the practice of continuous formative assessment with appropriate feedback that if executed properly, will lead to student ownership of the learning. These phases include:

1. Setting the Stage
2. Explanation
3. Modeling
4. Guided Practice
5. Independent Practice
6. Closure

Of course, in order to employ the six stages, a teacher must complete the overall curriculum unit planning prior to constructing the individual lessons. As discussed in Chapter Two, designing a lesson by aligning curriculum, instruction, and assessment is essential for student achievement.

THE PHASES OF DIRECT INSTRUCTION

Phase 1: Setting The Stage

In this stage, the teacher will describe what the students will be able to do successfully at the end of the lesson. As a reminder from Chapter Two, educators must unpack any content standard (describing what students are to be taught) and develop a KUD (what to know, understand, do) around the standard. This clarity of understanding at this stage will activate student's prior knowledge and connect the new learning to it.

Graphic organizers are an exemplary activity to help students access prior knowledge, as well as understand the sources from which they gathered that knowledge (a form of metacognition). A graphic organizer will permit the students to recognize the information they already know, and the activity assists the teacher in Setting the Stage to access the students' prior knowledge, leading them to connect it to new learning.

The following example is a type of graphic organizer that mimics the structure of how a photograph or drawing might be "framed."

"A stage setting is not a background; it is an environment."
~Robert Edmond Jones

© Debra Kennedy and Angela Smith (2016),
Student-Owned Learning: It's more than the teaching; it's about the learning

Instructions for the Frame of Reference Graphic Organizer:

- The topic is placed in the center of the organizer where a picture would be placed in a frame.

- Students individually write down words or phrases that come to mind when they think about this topic. These words go around the topic in the mat area of the frame.

- Students then write down how they came to know about this topic. These thoughts go outside of the mat in the framed area.

- Students share their graphic organizers with a partner or small group.

Phase 2: Explanations

Lecture is one of the oldest methods in teaching. The act of lecturing is valuable when information is not available in a text, when particular points need to be emphasized, or when the relationship among different points of view need clarification. When using lecture as a teaching method, educators must not lecture any more minutes than the students' ages. For example, when speaking to eight-year-olds, you have eight minutes before the students lose attention. This rule is true when speaking with anyone, even adults, and twenty minutes is the maximum time that most adults can attend in one sitting.

> "The whole purpose of education is to turn mirrors into windows."
> ~Sydney J. Harris

When addressing an entire class, you should employ some type of accountability tool that does not embarrass students by putting them on the spot, but that keeps the students tuned in to the important information. One particular tool often used widely is accountability sticks. These can simply be popsicle sticks with each student's name written on them and placed in a holder. Instead of asking for volunteers, you pull a stick, and the student whose name appears gets to answer the question or passes to a friend. After selecting a name, you should place the stick back into the jar in order to hold the anticipation that a student could be called upon again. Currently, with computers and smart phones available, you can try one of the many apps that randomly generate students' names. These are fun to display to students' names on a projector.

When planning the Explanation Phase of direct instruction, you must continuously check students' understanding to ascertain whether they are attending to the information. Robert Marzano in his work *Classroom Instruction That Works: Research-Based Strategies for Increasing Student Achievement* offers several protocols for effective summarizing and note-taking so that teachers can encourage students to analyze a subject and put the material into their own words. When students produce their own summary of new material, they will develop a more in-depth understanding of the content.

Another proven technique in the education world is the interactive notebook, which promotes students' processing of new material as they take notes on "home" side of the page and use the opposite side of the page to make meaning through a variety of methods. The following directions describe the preparation for an interactive notebook.

"The only thing more expensive than education is ignorance."
~Benjamin Franklin

Interactive Notebook Instructions:

- Students obtain an 8 ½ " x 11" spiral notebook with at least 100 pages.

- The students divide their notebook pages down the middle by drawing a line. On the right (home) side of the page, the students record the important information that the teacher disclosed in the lecture.

- Train students in note-taking by identifying the ideas that the students should write in their notebooks during the lecture or by providing templates that the students can glue in their notebook and then complete during the lecture.

- The student leaves the left (reflection) side of the page blank to record ideas or thoughts that assist with the processing and reflection of the information they recorded during the lecture.

"Words are but pictures of our thoughts."
~John Dryden

- After a few minutes of lecturing, give the students reflection time to summarize or question the information by writing their thoughts on the left (reflection) side of the page. This action allows processing time for the students, and it keeps the teacher from lecturing too long.

- Variations for interactive notebooks:
  - For primary students, you can have the students paste a poem on the right side of the page, and they draw pictures of what the poem means on the left side.
  - Students collect news clippings to connect to the lecture on reflection side.

o   Teacher gives students questions to answer on the reflection side to evoke deeper thinking.

Phase 3: Modeling

John Hollingsworth and Silvia Ybarra in their book, *Explicit Direct Instruction*, explain that modeling is not about showing students how to solve a problem; it is about revealing what a person is thinking as he or she solves the problem:

> Modeling is one of the most powerful methods of teaching because you are very clearly revealing the strategic thinking that is used to do something. The reason you do this is so that your students can copy your thinking and use the same approach when they do problems. (102)

The best technique to show students how individuals think through a process is the think-aloud approach. Often this technique is described as "eavesdropping on someone else's thinking."

Think-Aloud Instructions:

Read a passage aloud as the students listen. Pause at strategic points to demonstrating your thinking—stating ideas aloud, such as the following:

- Connections to previous information
- Images being visualized
- Problems with understanding the words or material
- Ways to fix the problems

Phase 4: Guided Practice

Practice makes perfect is a cliché, but in education some have revised this saying as perfect practice makes perfect meaning; in other words, when practicing new learning, the students must continuously determine through feedback that they are progressing properly to develop accurate knowledge. Most teachers are familiar with the Gradual Release of Responsibility Model. This protocol upholds the idea that the learning and the cognitive load <u>should be shifted to students</u> over time through teacher modeling, collaborative practice, and individual application. After the "I do" stage where the teacher models the skill, the gradual shift is to move into the "we do" stage where teacher and student work through the skill or problem together. This stage is teacher-guided so that students can gain enough correct practice through feedback that they will be able to finally move to the "you do" stage, the independent practice.

The Fist-to-Five technique is a solid method to make students conscious of their understanding during the guided practice phase of direct instruction.

Fist to Five Instructions:

- Ask students to show their level of understanding.
- Each student responds by showing a fist or a number of fingers that corresponds to their understanding of the concept:

> "An ounce of practice is worth more than tons of preaching."
> ~Gandhi

Fist to Five instructions (continued):

> - <u>Fist</u>: I don't understand; I need more help before I can begin.
> - <u>1 Finger</u>: I still need to discuss certain parts of the assignment.
> - <u>2 Fingers</u>: I am more comfortable with the assignment but would like to discuss more of the details.
> - <u>3 Fingers</u>: I do not totally understand, but I feel comfortable to start.
> - <u>4 Fingers</u>: I feel like I have a good handle on most parts of the assignment.
> - <u>5 Fingers</u>: I totally understand what to do.

Phase 5: Independent Practice

Once the lesson is taught and learned, it is time to practice independently. Independent practice is not about students teaching themselves or filling the time until the end of a class period. It is about providing the students with purposeful practice and repetition so they will possess the learning.

Before presenting a technique for the phase of independent practice, you need to review a basic explanation of memory. People have two types of memory: short-term and long-term. With short-term memory, information is stored for quick retrieval, but the information placed there does not remain for long because it is not practiced. For example, a person might look up the phone number for the pizza shop, yet after he or she calls in the order, the number is forgotten.

"Initiate a habit of choosing thoughts and ideas that support feeling good and powerful, and that elevate you to a higher consciousness."

~Wayne Dyer

With long-term memory though, the information is stored in the brain, and even though it may take a bit longer to call up, it is there for good because it has been elaborately repeated and practiced. The extra practice with the information stored in the long-term memory helps students build fluency with the new knowledge, and it builds speed and accuracy. For example, a child memorizing the Pledge of Allegiance repeats the words over and over, and eventually this pledge is easily retrieved from the long term memory. Extra practice such as homework should not be for students to learn content. The teacher should have delivered the content already. The purpose of practice is to move the teacher-presented content into a long-term storage in the brain. One method that helps promote long-term learning is called Sort Cards.

> "Practice isn't the thing you do once and you're good. It's the thing you do that makes you good."
> ~Malcom Gladwell

Sort Cards Instructions:

- Either individually or in small groups, students generate words, phrases, and/or definitions around a topic and place these on separate index cards. (Alternative: provide students a set of index cards with words or phrases around a topic.)

- Students sort the ideas into categories. The students may create their own categories, or the teacher may suggest the categories.

- When the sorting of the cards is complete, the students travel around the room to review and analyze the work of other groups.

- Students return to their team and process how other groups sorted their cards and consider resorting their cards into different categories.

Phase 6: Closure

As the lesson finishes, the students come away feeling successful with the learning objectives and have a sense of personal and relevant meaning about the content. The manner in which you wrap everything together will determine how much and how long the students will think about the material after the day's lesson is complete. Closure differs from evaluation, which is addressed in the next chapter. As a lesson is closed, you should consider the quality of the learning that has taken place and how it will be remembered for the future. You can conclude lessons in many ways, and the following are some favorites:

Closure Techniques:

- Email Hotline: Students type an email to their parents about their learning to discuss at home.

- Bumper Sticker: Students create a bumper sticker of the key ideas of the lesson.

- $2.00 Summary: Students write an idea about each concept on pieces of paper that say "worth ten cents;" they do this until they get twenty, or $2.00 worth.

- Elevator Speech: Students write a speech about the material that they can tell to someone while riding on a 30-second elevator ride.

- Mind Map: Students create a visual of what they have learned by connecting concepts in a graphic organizer starting from a center topic and extending outward.

"Education is for improving the lives of others and for leaving your community and world better than you found it."
~Marian Wright Edelman

© Debra Kennedy and Angela Smith (2016),
Student-Owned Learning: It's more than the teaching; it's about the learning

- Speed Recall: Students form two lines facing each other. The teacher asks a question and the two students facing each other discuss the answer. Every thirty seconds a bell signals one line to move to the right creating new partners for the next question.

- Snow Storm: Students write a two to four sentence summary of the learning. All students are told to crumble up paper (making a "snowball"), and they throw them into the middle of the room. Students grab a snowball and take turns reading another student's summary.

Designing one of the direct instruction lessons described here requires you to scrutinize each phase of the plan to ensure that all parts include engaging techniques. Direct Instruction is about the designing and the delivery of the content; it is not about the teacher lecturing. If you are to become an expert at direct instruction, then you must practice designing curriculum around the phases, while building a repertoire of instructional techniques to support the student-owned learning. It is only when you stick to a strategy and monitor the results of the student achievement that you can climb out of the implementation dip and inspire genuine student-owned learning.

"Never discourage someone who continually makes progress, no matter how slow."
~Plato

RECIPROCAL TEACHING

Face it: every educator is a teacher of reading. If education's true goal is to have students become learners on their own and much knowledge is gleaned through the process of reading, then, teachers are obligated to teach techniques that will strengthen students' reading skills.

> "Every educator is a teacher of reading."
>
> ~Deb Kennedy and Angela Smith

Reciprocal Teaching is an excellent strategy to increase students' comprehension of material, collaboration ability, and thinking skills. Annemarie Palincsar, co-founder of Reciprocal Teaching set out to discover the best manner to aid students who could read, as far as decoding the words, but who could not comprehend what they had read. From this doctoral study, she found that when instructors teach strategies of predicting, questioning, summarizing, and clarifying, they equip students with the tools to construct meaning.

Imagine the scenario from earlier in this chapter—the artist character builds a memory vessel for the information. Now, imagine no artist were available to create a memory vessel. This is what occurs when a student reads a text but makes no sense of the words; struggling readers face this anguish every day in all content areas. By instructing the strategy of Reciprocal Teaching, teachers can equip students with tools to construct meaning from their reading. If an instructor teaches and uses the four areas of Reciprocal Teaching regularly, then those will become automatic methods that students will turn to when they encounter material that does not make sense to them.

The facets of Reciprocal Teaching, **predicting, questioning, clarifying**, and **summarizing**, are listed in this order below; they do not have to be taught in any particular order, however. After students are comfortable with each of the four parts, using Reciprocal Teaching with assigned reading encourages students to monitor their own thinking and become actively involved in comprehending the content of the reading.

Predicting:

Prediction is a protocol that (skilled readers) employ when they tackle a text. Prediction helps students connect their personal experiences and prior knowledge to guess what may occur in the reading. As an important part of reading, prediction actively engages the reader to discover the text's meaning by continuously revising or confirming previous guesses about the reading.

Teachers should model a prediction protocol by drawing attention to the sequence of events in a text. Phase 3 of Direct Instruction mentioned earlier in the chapter describes the think-aloud strategy, and this technique is also one of the best protocols to teach predicting. The modeling of a prediction protocol needs to be used regularly through each school year to help students gain valuable reading comprehension skills and critical thinking skills. And, as students become more proficient, they can justify their predictions by supporting them with evidence from the text.

Several excellent books have been dedicated to the subject of literacy across the curriculum, and several are listed in the appendix of the book. Kylene Beers and Robert Probst are two educators who describe a myriad of prediction protocols that they have both used in their action research with students and have documented in their book: *Notice and Note* and *Reading Nonfiction.*

One method that Beers and Probst often recommend for predicting is a pre-reading activity in which the teachers provide the students with ten to fifteen random words from the text. Once the students read the words, they have to pull them together by coherently

Active

"A child who reads will be an adult who thinks."
~Unknown

Model it!
I wonder what would happen if . . . .

"Reading furnishes the mind only with materials of knowledge. It is thinking that makes what we read ours."
~John Locke

writing a sentence or two using all of the words. This activity helps the students to "predict" the subject and information in the upcoming reading assignment.

When the teacher has taught several methods of prediction, the students will be able to employ it in the Reciprocal Teaching process.

Questioning:

When instructing the parts of Reciprocal Teaching, educators must recognize the importance of instructing students to use questioning techniques. Students must understand the significance of being a "healthy skeptic," and that they cannot just accept everything at face value. People who do not question are easily duped into accepting information that may not necessarily be true or accurate.

Students need to understand that the act of questioning is about getting the correct information. This is especially germane when using informational text. Questioning techniques can easily be modeled when utilizing an Internet publication. You can instruct students to find information on the Internet by typing a question into a search engine. You can model how to find complete information by typing in strong or open-ended question. Also, you can show how to find the wrong information by asking a poorly-worded or closed question.

Another excellent protocol for question was developed by the librarians at California State University at Chico, and it is called the CRAAP test. CRAAP is an acronym that many students find amusing,

"The important thing is to never stop questioning."
~Albert Einstein

but it is also a superb measure for judging the credibility of reading. The CRAAP acronym stands for:

- **Currency**—how timely is the information?
- **Relevancy**—how closely does the information align with the researcher's needs?
- **Authority**—who is the source of this information and is that person an expert on the subject?
- **Accuracy**—how reliable is the information?
- **Purpose**—what is the reason this information was published?

By having the students apply the CRAAP test, they decide readily about the credibility of the informational text that they are reading. Although the CRAAP test creators meant for these questions to determine the worthiness of websites, the CRAAP test can essentially be applied to most informational text, and this protocol gives the students a strong foundation for questioning information.

> "Judge a man by his questions, not by his answers."
> ~Voltaire

Additionally, when thinking about this phase of Reciprocal Teaching, you must consider that for students to become proficient in questioning, they must also be fluid thinkers and fluent readers. Becoming a fluid thinker and a fluent reader means that students recognize concepts and words quickly and accurately; it does not mean, however, that just because students can say the words at lightning speed that they understand what they have read. This is the reason other skills need to be taught alongside fluency. Tim Rasinski describes fluency in his article *Creating Fluent Readers*:

> Reading fluency has three important dimensions that build a bridge to comprehension. The first dimension is *accuracy in word decoding*. Readers must be able to sound out the words

[handwritten: minimal effort to decode]

in a text with minimal errors. In terms of skills, this dimension refers to phonics and other strategies for decoding words. The second dimension is *automatic processing*. Readers need to expend as little mental effort as possible in the decoding aspect of reading so that they can use their finite cognitive resources for meaning making (LaBerge & Samuels, 1974). The third dimension is what linguists call *prosodic reading* (Schreiber, 1980, 1991; Schreiber & Read, 1980). The reader must parse the text into syntactically and semantically appropriate units. If readers read quickly and accurately but with no expression in their voices, if they place equal emphasis on every word and have no sense of phrasing, and if they ignore most punctuation, blowing through periods and other markers that indicate pauses, then it is unlikely that they will fully understand the text. (2004, para. 5)

"The important thing is to never stop questioning."
~Albert Einstein

As it has been said by many educators, "There are no multiple choice questions in life." The purpose of questioning in Reciprocal Teaching is to develop rapid information processing skills needed for reading comprehension and fluid thinking. Modeling or think-aloud are effective strategies to help students understand how to develop the technique of questioning. Another questioning method is to supply students with a list of question stems. A link for question stems is in the Appendix. With a list of question stems, students can select the ones that they find most meaningful and apply them to the content. With this small support, your students will own their learning by selecting their questions.

Clarifying:

During the clarifying step in Reciprocal Teaching, students make sense of what they are reading. If a person is watching a movie and misses a part, he or she would simply hit rewind and watch it again to see what was missed. In reading, educators need to teach students to hit pause and go back and re-read or identify the vocabulary that is making the author's message difficult to comprehend; several experts have named this "close reading." Clarification or close reading is about monitoring what has been read and using methods to comprehend the meaning of the text. Clarification can sometimes be achieved by extending the questioning techniques to have a discussion over the text, and it can also be accomplished by recognizing the warnings that comprehension is not occurring.

Have you have ever driven somewhere in a car and realized that you reached your destination but did not recall what happened along the way? Struggling readers experience a similar situation when they read the words fluidly but do not comprehend the meaning. The role of the clarifying is to ensure that the meaning of the content is apparent. Teaching students the metacognitive tool of recognizing their comprehension problems is the first step to clarifying meaning.

Cris Tovani in her work *I Read It, But I Don't Get It* teaches students how to recognize when comprehension is breaking down by using the following signals:

1. The voice inside the reader's head isn't interacting with the text.
2. The camera inside the reader's head shuts off.

"The lack of clarity could put the brakes on any journey to success."
~Steve Maraboli

(handwritten margin note: CIA so clarify? / star)

3. The reader's mind begins to wander.

4. The reader can't remember what has been read.

5. Clarifying questions asked by the reader are not answered.

6. The reader encounters a character and has no recollection when that character was introduced. (p. 38)

(handwritten margin note: Talk about your images)

You can assist readers with clarifying by modeling the pictures that form in your mind when reading a passage. Read a short passage aloud with students and then discuss what images you imagined as you read the piece.

Another barrier to comprehension is lack of word knowledge. When students are having difficulties clarifying or deriving meaning from a text, vocabulary acquisition is often at fault. Vocabulary instruction and strategic vocabulary development is critical to prevent reading failure. Although this book will not delve into vocabulary instruction, teachers should review Marzano's work on effective vocabulary instruction, mentioned in the reference section.

> "Vocabulary is a matter of word-building as well as word-using."
> ~David Crystal

During Reciprocal Teaching, students need to be familiar with some methods in clarifying unfamiliar vocabulary. One of the first steps is to ask questions about unfamiliar words:

1. How is the word pronounced?

2. What does the word or phrase mean?

3. Can I tell what the word might mean by looking at the other words around it?

Other methods to improve clarifying vocabulary include:

1. _Context Clues_: reading more of the passage to see if other words provide clues to help clarify the meaning of the unknown word

2. _Synonym_: substituting in similar word to see if it makes sense

3. _Dissect the Word_: identifying the prefixes, suffixes, or root words inside the unknown word to figure it out

4. _Ask Someone:_ requesting assistance from another student to define the word (Collaboration is key to Reciprocal Teaching)

5. _Sticky Notes_: in order to keep the context of the passage, placing a sticky note in as a placeholder and returning to it later

6. _Connections:_ thinking about what the student already knows to see if it helps decipher the word, or thinking if the word appeared in another context

"The more you read, the more you know. The more you learn, the more places you will go."
-Dr. Suess

underlined come back

Beginning
Middle
End

Summarizing:

Summarizing is an essential skill to be able to break apart larger pieces into smaller parts while maintaining the integrity of the key points. Using as few words as possible to restate the main idea, summarizing can be done in writing, orally, through drama, through art and music, in groups and individually. Research supports summarizing as one of the most effective study strategies. Teachers should be warned, though: summarizing is also one of the hardest skills to teach to students.

Important but difficult

S WBST

A low risk method to help students understand the concept of summarizing is to have them orally review a movie or the events of a typical school day. Students should be reminded that summaries do not include opinions. You should continue the practice oral summaries of different events to keep students focusing in on the main idea, highlights, or important points.

When you wish to teach summarizing with a text, graphic organizers such as a plot map, can help students identify the characters and main events to summarize the story. In non-fiction texts, you need to instruct students on the skill of skimming for important facts to build understanding. The students should highlight key ideas, while crossing out non-essential pieces not needed in the summary.

"If you can't explain it simply, you don't understand it well enough."
~Albert Einstein

Pulling It Altogether:

Reciprocal Teaching requires educators to teach students how to predict, how to question, how to clarify, and how to summarize so that students can have meaningful conversations about the content. Once students truly own the four areas of Reciprocal Teaching, they will be able to use each part either independently or together. Teachers can design lessons around one or two of the parts; for example, the students can partner and brainstorm questions and share predictions, or the instructor can use all four pieces in more specific situations, such as Learning Circles. The Learning Circle approach, sometimes called Literature Circles in the language arts classroom, is a cooperative learning technique that involves assigning each team member a role to investigate the text in with a particular purpose.

As with any worthwhile cooperative learning method, a teacher should implement this approach by demonstrating what each role might look and sound like; after each role's actions are established, the teacher should have a group of students simulate a Learning Circle while the rest of the class observes and gives feedback over the roles and process. The student feedback is crucial at this point in that it allows students to become familiar with the Learning Circle protocol, and more importantly, it empowers students to become independent thinkers instead of relying on the teacher's feedback.

This transition from teacher-led instruction to student-owned learning requires practice and competency in all techniques. Once the students have grown enough to where you can shift from the role of instructor to coach, the class will clear the implementation dip and advance to student-owned learning. Implementing the Learning Circle protocol will do just that.

> "The dictionary is the only place where success comes before work."
> ~Mark Twain

The Learning Circle:

- Assign a common text that the students read individually.
- Place students in groups of five and assign a role to the students or have the students select a role.
- Each group then engages in a discussion about the text using the assigned roles:
  - The Project Manager develops a list of questions for the group to discuss. He or she focus on the big ideas of the text and the personal reactions to the content. (This the questioning aspect of Reciprocal Teaching.)
  - The Connector helps the group to make connections to real life and the content. (This is the clarifying facet of Reciprocal Teaching.)

- o The Passage Master identifies interesting or confusing parts of the text. (This also involves clarifying, but it can also involve predicting and questioning aspects of Reciprocal Teaching.)

- o The Illustrator draws images that capture the group's thoughts about the reading. (In Reciprocal Teaching, the illustrator is assisting with clarifying the text.)

- o The Reporter prepares a summary of the group's discussion of the material to report to the class. (This is the aspect of summarizing in Reciprocal Teaching.)

- After the members of the group have exhausted their role, the reporters from each group will share the group's findings with the entire class. This activity allows for a culmination of the activity and a review of the text.

    - o Variation: Jigsaw the text. In a jigsaw, select the groups for the Learning Circles before assigning the reading. Then, charge each Learning Circle with a different text passage. After the students read their passage, they engage in their roles in the Learning Circle. When the Learning Circles are complete, and it is time for each Reporter to speak, every student must take notes on the information that the Reporter shares since each group read a different passage. This variation encourages more accountability and student-owned learning.

*As an added variation for different subject areas, the above roles could be changed. In a science room, for example, one might include a scientist, a tool gatherer, an organizer, etc.

CONCLUSION

Metacognition is the process of thinking about one's own learning. Students who become stuck in the implementation dip need methods to help lead them to construct their own learning. Direct Instruction and Reciprocal Teaching are proven strategies that envelop many active learning techniques to engage students in absorbing any content. Teachers who choose a high impact strategy and adhere to it will see student achievement soar. Effective instruction requires both a concentrated effort in designing lessons, as well as deliberate planning in the delivery of the instruction to produce high academic rigor and retention.

"Collaboration is the new competition."
~David Amerland

REFLECTION QUESTIONS

1. How do you get your students to begin thinking about how they learn?
1. What learning qualities would you like to see in students?
2. How much time do you spend planning your lessons?
3. How do you keep updated on the latest research?
4. What is your "go-to" strategy, and how do you know that it is producing high rigor and retention?
5. Who does most of the work during your lessons? You? Students?
6. Every day, does every student read, write, speak, listen, and think during the lesson?

REFERENCES

Beers, K. & Probst, R. (2015) *Reading nonfiction: Notice & note stances, signposts, and strategies*. Portsmouth, NH: Heinemann.

Hattie, J. (2012). *Visible learning for teachers: Maximizing impact on learning*. London, England: Routledge.

Hollingsworth, J. & Ybarra, S. (2009). *Explicit direct instruction: The power of the well-crafted, well-taught lesson*.

Marzano, R. J., Pickering, D., & Pollock, J. E. (2001). *Classroom instruction that works: Research-based strategies for increasing student achievement*. Alexandria, VA: Association for Supervision and Curriculum Development. Thousand Oaks, CA: Corwin Press.

Meriam Library. (2010) *Evaluating information—applying the CRAAP test*. California State University, Chico. Retrieved from https://www.csuchico.edu/lins/handouts/eval_websites.pdf

Palinscar, A. S. & Brown, A. L. (1984). Reciprocal teaching of comprehension-fostering and comprehension-monitoring strategies. *Cognition and Instruction*. 1(2), 117-175.

Rasinki, T. (2004) Creating fluent readers. *Educational Leadership*. 61(6), 46-51.

Tovani, C. (2000). *I read it, but I don't get it: Comprehension strategies for adolescent readers*. Portland, ME: Stenhouse Publishers.

Wiggins, G. P., McTighe, J., Kiernan, L. J., Frost, F., & Association for Supervision and Curriculum Development. (1998). *Understanding by design*. Alexandria, VA: Association for Supervision and Curriculum Development.

Table 5.1

Theme	Explanation	Importance
Assessment	As discussed in Chapter Two, assessment is the process of documenting a student's understanding as a way to gauge and improve teaching and learning.	Assessments are an integral part of the instructional process. These are ongoing non-graded checkpoints with the purpose of improving learning and teaching.
Evaluation	Evaluation focuses on grades and gauges the final quality by judging the overall product and to provide learning through a grade or score.	Evaluations are used to determine if the educational goals have been met. They exhibit if the students are learning the skills or knowledge, and they allow the teacher to analyze if the instruction has been appropriate.
Feedback	Feedback provides students with timely constructive comments, criticisms, corrections, content, and/or elaborations to keep them moving forward in their learning.	Feedback is an inherent part of learning. Feedback through assessment provides student clear guidance on improving their learning. Appropriate feedback increases students perceptions of self-efficacy and promotes intrinsic interest in the task at hand.
Goal Setting	Goal setting is an action plan that motivates and guides a student toward a set criteria for improvement.	Goal setting helps build self-confidence and increases students' motivation to achieve higher goals.
Instructional Communication	Instructional communication is the act of setting a clear framework so the students can completely meet the goals of the lesson.	Teachers must have a strong command of the content to be competent classroom communicators. If they muddy the material, the students will not understand the intentions of the lesson and will not be successful in their learning goal.
Rubrics	Rubrics are evaluation tools that include the criteria being assessed for an assignment.	Rubrics provide a clear description of what is expected in an assignment. The rubric allows students to see exactly what they need to do to master the goals of the activity, project, or performance.

THE STUDENT "WHY?"

During any given lesson, a typical student might ask, "Will this be on the test?" John Green, one of the founders of the popular YouTube learning series, *Crash Course*, has a wonderful answer that urges student-owned learning:

> Yeah, about the test . . . The test will measure whether you are an informed, engaged, and productive citizen of the world, and it will take place in schools and bars and hospitals and dorm rooms and in places of worship. You will be tested on first dates, in job interviews, while watching football, and while scrolling through your Twitter feed. The test will judge your ability to think about things other than celebrity marriages, whether you'll be easily persuaded by empty political rhetoric, and whether you'll be able to place your life and your community in a broader context. The test will last your entire life, and it will be comprised of the millions of decisions that, when taken together, will make your life yours. And everything,
>
> everything, will be on it. I know, right? So pay attention. (2012, 0:15)

"The test will measure whether you are an informed, engaged, and productive citizen of the world . . ."

~John Green

ASSESSMENT OR EVALUATION

Often when teachers begin their careers, they see assessment as a prodigious, singular event: the test. In fact, though, assessment is part and parcel of the entire instructional process. As discussed briefly in Chapter Two, assessment is a process that begins before the instruction, continues during the instruction, and occurs after the lesson has ended. Its purpose is to provide check-ups for the students and the teacher to determine if and how much learning has occurred.

Assessment should guide all decision-making in the instructional process, for it is the umbrella under which feedback, goal-setting, and evaluation reside. Assessment is not "the" test; assessment does not even have to involve grades because in reality, it is a tool to actuate understanding—the method by which the teacher and the student gauge the learning.

Often, assessment and evaluation are used synonymously when they actually are two different processes. As mentioned in the previous paragraph, assessment is the on-going feedback that helps to guide students to their next level and sometimes out of the implementation dip. Evaluation, on the other hand, is about making inferences or judgments about the learning. Evaluation must be used carefully in the classroom setting, and teachers must take caution when employing evaluation tools to make inferences about students. Since instructors are just sampling the learning that has taken place, they must not confuse the students' intelligence with what the students gained from the learning. For example, when most people turn sixteen years of age in Ohio, they go to the local Bureau of Motor Vehicles (BMV) to take a driver's permit test. This test asks a few questions about traffic laws and what to do in a few driving situations. Of course, not enough room or time exists to ask a question about every occasion one might encounter when driving. Basically, the test is a sampling of driving experiences, and these driving questions evaluate whether the 16-year-old is ready to practice driving. The BMV officials make an inference based on the driving test score. Sometimes those inferences are good, but occasionally, they may be flawed. Once the teen has passed the written test and practices driving to obtain the required

> "A good teacher can inspire hope, ignite imagination, and instill a love of learning."
> ~Brad Henry

number of rehearsal hours, he or she returns to the BMV for the in-car assessment. The licensing official rides with the teen around a few blocks, and once again, based on a minimal evaluation, the instructor makes an inference to grant a driver's license to this teen that will allow him or her to drive anywhere in the United States and possibly in other countries. Depending upon the location of the driving test, the sampling may have been on a two-way rural town road, an inner-city Chicago street, or California's Grapevine Interstate. The point is that teachers need to be careful when using evaluations that only include a sampling of the material to make inferences about the future of the students. Though many districts require a certain number of grades based on a rigid timeline under the guise of being fair to students, it is imperative that teachers design evaluation that is in direct alignment to the learning objective.

DOK REVISITED

Back in Chapter Two, a graphic organizer showed a look at standards in relation to the Depth of Knowledge (DOK) level (see Table 5.2), and each test question was placed on the graphic organizer to ensure that the rigor was at the correct level. Another reason to display the standard and the rigor level graphically is to ensure alignment from the standard to the test. With this method, a teacher is forming a plan right from the beginning of the unit to ensure that the sampling is actually aligned, thus ensuring the accurate inferences about students' learning.

Table 5.2

Standard	DOK 1	DOK 2	DOK 3	DOK 4
Analyze how a text makes connections among and distinctions between individuals, ideas, or events (e.g., through comparisons, analogies, or categories).		Q. 1-2	Analyze Q. 3-5	
Determine an author's point of view or purpose in a text and **analyze** how the author acknowledges and responds to conflicting evidence or viewpoints.		Determine Q. 6-9	Analyze Q. 10-16	
Write narratives to develop real or imagined experiences or events using effective technique, relevant descriptive details, and well-structured event sequences.				Write Q.16-25

LEVELS OF FEEDBACK

Whether using an evaluation at the end of a unit or employing specific assessments throughout a unit, an important component for student learning is the feedback. Research has proven what teachers have known for years, that giving students meaningful feedback leads to increased learning. Feedback is even more powerful when the teacher and students have positive rapport. Educational research demonstrates that all feedback, however, is not equal, and some types may have a negative impact on student learning. John Hattie and Helen Timperley in their article, "The Power of Feedback" address the most effective ways to use feedback:

> "A goal without a plan is just a wish."
> ~Unknown

1. *Be specific in giving feedback:* The teacher commentary must help students accrue the skills to reach their next level learning goal. Phrases, such as "Great Job" or "Nice Work," are a form of praise and do not provide students with the necessary information that they need to continue their learning.

2. *Just-in-time feedback:* Studies have shown that giving immediate or timely feedback is much more effective than waiting days, weeks, or months.

3. *Feedback toward the goal:* Student learning is on a continuum, and they should always be aware of their next learning goal. The intention of feedback is to assist students in reaching their next level.

Dr. Hattie further defines the four types of feedback in his book, *Visible Learning for Teachers*:

1. Praise level *[handwritten: Be Specific]*
2. Task level *[handwritten: Use a? - How could you....]*
3. Process level
4. Self-regulation level (pp. 133-136)

[handwritten margin notes: Formative assessment - activities / Summative → Do in K.U.D.]

In order to understand the difference in the levels, consider these types of feedback and then examine the level of the feedback.

PRAISE

First, a word of caution about the basic level of feedback, praise: those who have researched feedback agree that praise is an inferior form of feedback. In fact, Carol Dweck reveals that using praise as feedback provides students with a short burst of pride, followed by a long string of negative consequences. Carol Dweck's research on fixed and growth mindsets shows "that educators cannot hand students confidence on a silver platter by praising their intelligence" (p. 39). Dweck cautions teachers to praise students on their effort rather than their intelligence. For example, "I like the way that you tried all of your protocols to find the best answer to the question," or "You really studied hard for the science test by outlining all of the key details. Your extra work really worked!"

FEEDBACK

According to Hattie, the first level of feedback, praise, must focus on effort, rather than the statements such as "kiss your brain," which imply that the students' learning is fixed by what is inside of them. When praise feedback is properly administered, by citing effort rather than intelligence, the students realize that the brain needs exercise just like the muscles in their bodies. This metacognition, or type of learning about how a person learns, is what cultivates the motivation to continue learning. For example, "You really worked hard today and look what you've accomplished!"

"Make feedback normal, not a performance review."
~Ed Batista

A second type of feedback, task level, corrects students' misconceptions. Feedback at the task or product level is powerful for gaining information and surface knowledge. This type of feedback is generally used on new tasks or new units to direct the thinking toward correct actions. The most common situation is a teacher asking questions to the entire class and then giving specific feedback to correct or direct their attention to particular content. Math facts or grammar exercises often produce this type of task feedback. For example, "So your answer is not correct here. You need to use these steps to solve this problem."

Once beyond the right or wrong of the task, teachers must move deeper by instructing students to identify ways to develop more effective protocol usage. Hattie names this type of feedback process level. As mentioned earlier, feedback is more effective when it is given as an ongoing method instead of at the end of the learning. Examples of feedback at this level include, "You are asked to look at these two authors, how are they alike and how are they different?" or "What method could you use to find the meaning of the word that is giving you trouble?"

The highest level of feedback, according to Hattie, is when teachers guide the students to monitor their own learning process. The self-regulation level provides the confidence to go deeper in the task. Essentially, the teacher asks the student probing questions to prompt metacognition in the student. The questions should be open-ended and lead students to draw conclusions about their learning. For example, "You work on that story was definitely in the right direction. What other ways might you end it?"

> "The aim is to provide feedback that is 'just in time,' and 'just what I need to help me move forward.'"
> ~John Hattie

Table 5.3 gives concise examples of the levels of feedback:

Table 5.3

Actual feedback	Praise	Task	Process	Self-regula-tion
Good job, Brooke!	X			
What do you place at the end of a sentence?		X		
The last time you solved the equation, you solved for X. Look at this problem again, and think about what we discussed.			X	
Do you think you met the criteria for an "A"?				X
How could you use the exemplar to help you structure your work?			X	
What strategy could you use to check your accuracy of your answers?			X	
You put a "six" for this answer. It should have been a "five".		X		
Thanks, Deke. You worked really hard today.	X			
You really need to put in a lot more effort. This is disappointing.	This is negative feedback.			
It might have helped, if you had done your reading over the weekend.	This is sarcasm.			

In order to obtain the highest feedback level with students, you must start by teaching them the different types of feedback previously explained. If the students are capable of capturing your feedback, then you should instruct them on how to chart it. This type of activity helps students become more self-aware and provides you with essential information on the variety of feedback you are giving. An added layer to this exercise would be for you to demonstrate the difference between praise and feedback so that the students can differentiate the two when they are charting.

> "The highest level of feedback is when teachers guide the students to monitor their own learning."
> ~John Hattie

In reviewing Table 5.3, you should set a goal to chart feedback for one week to see the most common level of feedback being provided to the students. You should share this goal with the students: this aids in the students seeing their teacher as a learner.

This charting exercise can lead to teaching students how and why to set their own learning goals. By setting goals, students can:

1. Improve their academic performance
2. Increase their self-confidence
3. Bolster their motivation to grow and learn

THE BASICS OF GOAL-SETTING

A significant difference exists between setting a goal so a person can say that he or she did something and setting a goal with a specific action plan to monitor the progress along the way. You must help students to understand that a goal is an end target that requires a thoughtful plan of action.

This can be taught to students in a three-step process:

1. Develop a realistic goal
2. Create a step-by-step action plan
3. Reflect on the progress

Step One: Develop a realistic goal

SMART goals have been established for many years, but here is a review of the acronym:

- o **S** = Specific
- o **M** = Measurable
- o **A** = Attainable
- o **R** = Relevant, Rigorous, Realistic, and Results Focused
- o **T** = Timely and Trackable

> "The victory of success is half won when one gains the habit of setting and achieving goals."
>
> ~Og Mandino

While it is not easy to write goals in the SMART format, it is a good idea to create them as detailed and realistically as possible. When students are asked to write a goal, they may write something like, "I will get an A in math class." This may be a good start for a student who excels in math, but the overall goal is too broad and must be narrowed down and clearly defined. A more refined goal might look like this:

> "I will bring all of my materials to math class, look over my notes before class, complete homework each night, and correct any missed problems for the entire nine weeks in order to bring my grade up on my report card."

You should encourage students to think through what they are trying to achieve and include actionable steps to move them toward that end goal.

Step Two: Create a step-by-step action plan

You should coach students to compose a timeline with specific mini-goals to achieve toward the main goal. Using the previously mentioned math example, students could develop a timeline based on each week of the grading period:

✓

Table 5.4

Timeline	Action Step	Reflection Notes
Week One	Come Prepared to Class	
Week Two	Review Notes Prior to Class	
Week Three	Homework Complete	
Week Four	Corrected Problems	

Step Three: Reflect on the progress

Your key objective in teaching goal-setting is to help the students understand that the journey to reach the goal is as important or even more important than the goal itself. Too often, students, teachers, and parents only focus on the end result: the grade. In order to recognize the perseverance, hard work, and determination, it is imperative for you to help students understand the magnitude of self-reflection. Whether it is done daily or weekly, the habit of reflecting on progress is necessary to encourage favorable goal setting. One easy method of guiding students to reflect is by building in reflection moments throughout a class period. As discussed in Chapter Four, students have difficulty paying attention for a length of time. After each concept or skill is presented, you should request the students to think about what they just learned and if time permits, have them share the information with a neighbor. This exercise prepares students to reflect on their own. When they have completed a step in their action plan, you must require that the students compose a short

"People with goals succeed because they know where they're going."
~Earl Nightingale

Turn+Talk!

explanation of how he or she reached that step in the plan. Their explanation allows the students to reflect upon their journey to the ultimate goal. Moreover, when the students learn how to reflect, the parent question of "What did you do in school today?" will not be answered with "nothing" because the students will have information to report from the reflection on their new learning. Mindfulness of new learning comes through reflection of that learning. For further study in mindfulness of learning, the book, *Learning and Leading Habits of Mind* by Art Costa and Bena Kallick provides many techniques for reflection.

INSTRUCTIONAL COMMUNICATION

The classroom, a microcosm of a social structure, is a group of students from different socioeconomic background, cultures, and cognitive abilities. The main task for this microcosm is to learn the given content; the lynch pin for this socialization and learning to occur is the teacher, the expert. During instruction, the main intention is for you to challenge students with new information and knowledge. Before you can build a culture of collaboration among a group of disparate individuals, you must possess adequate knowledge of the subject matter and be able to design activities that communicate the message effectively. You must have the ability to persuade the students to accept the new ideas while orchestrating a classroom atmosphere with meaningful social interactions.

Communication in the classroom is more than just the transmission and reception of messages. If education were about providing surface knowledge only, then the process of just transmitting information would be acceptable during the lesson. Answering questions by using Google is a good example of the transmission of information.

> "Teachers who promote reflective classrooms ensure that students are fully engaged in the process of making meaning."
> ~Art Costa

Decidedly though, Google-searched information has little long-term meaning for the receiver, and the same could be said for the classroom where the instructor spews facts with little connection or context.

On the other hand, instructional communication occurs when the teacher provides meaningful information in a manner that connects those ideas for students and allows them to incorporate that new learning into their own schema. In the classroom setting, instructional communication is giving students the tools to build their own meaningful knowledge, as opposed to the mere transmission of information that does little to build student knowledge.

How can you become a master of instructional communication? As discussed previously in Chapter Two, you must have a command of the standards and curriculum to discern fully what the students need to know, understand, and do. Additionally, you must be able to deliver this information in a student-friendly manner so that students can connect with the information personally, thus making them to lead their own making learning.

To be a strong instructional communicator, you must consider the purpose of an activity or evaluation from its very beginnings. Furthermore, you must always consider how your students think. The primary question from students is always, "Why?"—"Why do I need to know this? Why do I need to do this? Why? Why? Why?" If you can answer the why to every statement and activity, then you are on the path to becoming a a competent instructional communicator because you have a strong grasp of the content, and thus, will be able to lead students to significant learning.

INSTRUCTIONAL COMMUNICATION IN PRACTICE

For many years in education, the test at the end of the unit was the popular practice that teachers used to assess their students' skills and knowledge. Of course, a plethora of research has been conducted to demonstrate the disadvantages of this type of evaluation. For many years, Thomas Guskey has compelled educators to reform the grading process by dispelling myths about the end-game test and the competitive nature of the classroom. While the intention here is not to discuss these disadvantages, the work of Guskey, Ken O'Connor, and many others is critical to mention because at times, teachers will need to evaluate the amount of skill and/or knowledge that a student has accrued through a unit of study. As mentioned previously in this chapter, several steps must occur before the students take the culminating "test." By assessing the students informally during the instruction, by teaching goal-setting action plans and reflection, and by utilizing appropriate feedback, you will have led the students to the point where they are prepared for a summative assessment that demonstrates their mastery of the content.

One of the best methods for a summative assessment is to have the students complete a performance-based assignment. This type of assessment will allow students to synthesize and apply the skills and knowledge they have learned by creating a worthwhile product relevant and personal for them. The best performance-based evaluation is one that incorporates most of the skills and knowledge

> "I am a teacher. I inspire my students to follow their dreams, discover their creativity, interests, and talents, and learn to use them to their fullest potential."
> ~Unknown

dictated by the standards of the unit and provides students with a choice on how to demonstrate their understanding of those concepts. Grant Wiggins and Jay McTighe have written extensively about the use of performance-based assessments; consulting their work is helpful for generating ideas.

For the purposes of this chapter, let us return to the sample unit from Chapter Two: "Through My Eyes." The standards selected in this unit require the students to analyze text connections, determine author's point of view, and write narratives. If the unit is designed as discussed in Chapter Two, then the teacher has provided formative assessments and feedback along the way to determine the students' grasp of skills and knowledge, but now the teacher needs to judge if the students have comprehensively absorbed the standards of the unit by designing an evaluation that will exhibit this. This unit lends itself nicely to a performance-based assessment that allows the class to produce a collaborative work: a class book. The name of the class book is *Through My Eyes*, and it includes a narrative from each student in the class. Producing a class book has several advantages:

> "I am not a teacher, but an awakener."
> ~Robert Frost

1. It is a natural performance-based assessment because each student must compose his or her story.
2. It provides inherent accountability because the book will be published for the class, and everyone will have the opportunity to read each other's story.

As an instructional communicator, this teacher must coach the students to produce a stellar narrative by providing them with specific guidelines and rubric to help them display their learning of the skills and knowledge from the unit. This action begins with the teacher composing a set of instructions that he or she wants the students to follow, and then designing a rubric around the standards and the instructions of the assignment. When designing a set of instructions, the teacher must refer to the standards and decide upon the most important ones to evaluate in the summative assessment. As discussed in Chapter Two, if the teacher has included too many standards in the unit, the amount of skills and knowledge are overwhelming for the students, and the teacher will have difficulty in completely assessing all of them. In fact, the Common Core State Standards were designed to force students to delve deeply into a topic rather than memorizing superficial facts (Marzano, n.d., para. 5).

In reviewing the standards of "Through My Eyes," let's focus on standard #3:

Standard #3 W 8.3: Write narratives to develop real or imagined experiences or events using effective technique, relevant descriptive details, and well-structured event sequences.

    a. *Engage and orient the reader by establishing a context and point of view and introducing a narrator and/or characters; organize an event sequence that unfolds naturally and logically.*

Use narrative techniques, such as dialogue, pacing, description, and reflection, to develop experiences, events, and/or characters.

    b. *Use a variety of transition words, phrases, and clauses to convey sequence, signal shifts from one time frame or setting to another, and show the relationships among experiences and events.*

    c. *Use precise words and phrases, relevant descriptive details, and sensory language to capture the action and convey experiences and events.*

d. *Provide a conclusion that follows from and reflects on the narrated experiences or events.*

Up to the point of assigning the culminating evaluation, the teacher has formatively assessed the students on the standards, and from unpacking the standard, he or she has an understanding about which criteria to emphasize at the end of the unit. To prepare to make a class book and to include the important parts of Standard #3 W 8.3, the prompt for the summative assessment would look like this:

> Write about a real or imagined event that changed your attitude about something. Your narrative composition must include the following:

1. The plot of your story needs to have a clear beginning, middle, and end, and transition words must link the events together.

2. You may use first or third person point of view, and the point of view needs to be consistent.

3. The characters of story must be developed by providing specific details about them and their relationships with others.

4. The story needs to include properly punctuated dialogue between the characters.

5. The story must include descriptive details and use examples of sensory language.

6. The story must end with a reflective conclusion.

> "In a rational society, the best of us would aspire to be teachers and the rest of us would have to settle for something less."
> ~Lee Iococca

RUBRICS

Now that the criteria are set for the assignment, the teacher must design a rubric that incorporates the success criteria for the assignment and shows the students what they need to do to earn the highest grade for the narrative.

A note about rubrics: While it is tempting to use ready-made rubrics, teachers should be cautious in employing them. Master teachers will design their own rubrics to fit the exact assignment. That way, they know if their students are truly meeting the criteria of the standard. Many rubric-generating websites are available for teachers; unless though, the generator permits the teacher to include his or her own descriptors, the rubric will not comprehensively fit the assignment. Using a rubric not designed specifically for the summative assessment does a disservice to the students and teacher: the students are not really assessed on the exact skills and knowledge of the unit, and the teacher does not receive a clear picture of what the students gained from the unit.

"It's easy to make a buck. It's a lot tougher to make a difference."
~Tom Brokaw

Designing rubrics could be an entire course of study in itself, but for now, here are some simplified tips:

1. Design criteria-based rubrics (as opposed to holistic rubrics), as they provide the most feedback for students and teachers.
2. Take each criterion and make it a category on the rubric.
3. Divide each criterion into three levels: emerging, focused, student-owned.
4. Write descriptors that follow the standard for each criterion level.

Each level of the rubric should be an improvement over the last. The middle descriptor, the focused-level, should be the exact criterion. In the emerging descriptor, the student has omitted part or all of the criterion, and in the top descriptor, the student-owned level, the student has performed above the expectations of the criterion. For example, the first criterion of the assignment above is "The plot of your story needs to have a clear beginning, middle, and end, and transition words must link the events together." On the rubric, the indicators would look like these:

- **Emerging**: The plot of the story does not have a definite beginning, middle, or end, and/or few transition words link together the events.
- **Focused:** The plot of the story has a beginning, middle, and end, and an adequate transition words link the events of the story.
- **Student-owned**: The plot of the story has a definite, meaningful beginning, middle, and end, and descriptive, appropriate transition words link the events of the story.

This method of rubric design is a shift from some evaluation tools. Many rubric designers make their highest rubric level the criterion, and then the descriptors are reduced from there. If you truly want your students to lead their own learning though, you must provide stretch by challenging the students to exceed the criteria. For a more developed example, Table 5.4 is a rubric for the entire summative assessment, Through My Eyes.

"If I ran a school, I'd give the average grade to the ones who gave me all the right answers, for being good parrots. I'd give the top grades to those who made a lot of mistakes and told me about them, and then told me what they learned from them."
~Buckminster Fuller

Through My Eyes Narrative Rubric

Table 5.5

Criteria	Student-owned	Focused	Emerging
The plot of the story has a clear beginning, middle, and end, and transition words link the events together.	The plot of the story does not have a definite beginning, middle, or end, and/or few transition words link together the events.	The plot of the story has a beginning, middle, and end, and an adequate transition words link the events of the story.	The plot of the story has a definite, meaningful beginning, middle, and end, and descriptive, appropriate transition words link the events of the story.
The plot includes first or third person point of view and is consistent throughout the story.	The point of view is unclear and/or inconsistent.	The plot includes first or third person point of view consistently throughout the story.	The plot includes the most appropriate point of view for the story, and it is employed consistently.
The characters of story are developed with specific details and their relationships with others.	The characters of the story are not fully developed and/or the relationships with others is not obvious.	The characters of story are developed with specific details and their relationships between others is clear.	The characters of the story are fully developed with specific details, and the relationships with others are easily established for the reader.
The story includes properly punctuated dialogue between the characters.	The story includes little dialogue, and/or the dialogue is punctuated inaccurately.	The story includes properly punctuated dialogue between the characters.	The story includes strong dialogue that advances the plot, and it is punctuated accurately.
The story includes descriptive details and uses examples of sensory language.	The story includes few descriptive details and uses few or no examples of sensory language.	The story includes descriptive details and uses examples of sensory language.	The story includes excellent descriptive details and uses original examples of sensory language.
The story ends with a reflective conclusion.	The story ends abruptly with no reflective conclusion.	The story ends with a reflective conclusion.	The story ends with a reflective conclusion that leaves the reader with a message or call to action.

"Life's most persistent and urgent question is: What are you doing for others?"
~Martin Luther King, Jr.

A final thought about rubrics: though teacher subjectivity in evaluating a student's work is unavoidable, criterion-based rubrics assist in removing some of the subjectivity in grading a performance-based assessment. Rubrics provide clear guidelines and feedback, and though they are not the perfect evaluation tool, they are an immense improvement over putting a grade at the top of a test. Moreover, if used regularly, rubrics will promote student-owned learning because the students have clear guidelines to which they can aspire, and the rubric offers teachers the opportunity to provide self-regulation feedback, which research exhibits as the most meaningful type. Everybody wins when using rubrics: the teacher can evaluate the exact learning, and the student gains an understanding about the priorities of summative assessment.

CONCLUSION

Habit #2 of Stephen Covey's *Seven Habits of Highly Effective People* posits that if people want to reach goal, they need to imagine what that goal looks like. In other words, they must "begin with the end in mind." Essentially, teachers must do the same, if they truly want success for their students. By understanding the ongoing process of assessment, realizing the difference between assessment and evaluation, using purposeful feedback, teaching goal-setting, practicing exemplary instructional communication, and designing robust rubrics, you will be well on the way to pushing through the implementation dip and into a sterling classroom where the students take ownership of their learning. The ideas of this chapter are some of the most difficult in education to execute because you must be mindful of them at all moments of instruction. With a bit of practice, though, they can become part of your repertoire and will pay dividends the entire school year.

REFLECTION QUESTIONS

1. How do you know when students have mastered the content?

2. What evidence can you provide to prove that you have a growth mindset?

3. What was your last personal goal that you made for yourself? Did you achieve it?

4. How can you demonstrate to students that you are still a learner?

5. How do you know if your students truly understand your instructions?

REFERENCES

Costa, A. L., & Kallick, B. (2008). *Learning and leading with habits of mind: 16 essential characteristics for success.* Alexandria, VA: Association for Supervision and Curriculum Development.

Covey, S. R. (2004). *The 7 habits of highly effective people: Restoring the character ethic.* New York: Free Press.

Dweck, C. (2007). The perils and promise of praise. *Educational Leadership.* 65(2), 34-39. Retrieved from http://www.ascd.org/publications/educational-leadership/oct07/vol65/num02/The-Perils-and-Promises-of-Praise.aspx

Green, J. (2012, January 26) *The agricultural revolution: crash course world history #1.* [Video file]. Retrieved from https://www.youtube.com/watch?v=Yocja_N5s1I

Guskey, T. R. (2015). *On your mark: Challenging the conventions of grading and reporting.* Bloomington, IN: Solution Tree.

Hattie, J. (2012). *Visible learning for teachers: Maximizing impact on learning.* London, England: Routledge.

Hattie, J. & Timperley, H. (2007). The power of feedback. *Review of Educational Research.* 77(81), 81-112. Retrieved from http://education.qld.gov.au/staff/development/ performance/ resources/readings/power-feedback.pdf

Marzano, R. (n.d.) *Common core is a second order change: Understand it and thrive.* Common Core and the Art and Science of Teaching Series, Marzano Center. Retrieved from http://www.marzanocommoncore.com/

Wiggins, G., & McTighe, J. (2004). *Understanding by design professional development workbook.* Alexandria, VA: Association for Supervision and Curriculum Development.

STUDENT-OWNED LEARNING
CHAPTER SIX
THE HARD WORK OF PREPARING
A STUDENT-OWNED CLASSROOM

Preparing a student-owned classroom requires hard work. Becoming an expert teacher means really owning the material and tools necessary to impact students and lead them to their own learning. Mastering the art and science of teaching takes continual vigilance, and any time people develop new skills, the change requires perseverance and dedication. As an educator, our job is to teach students how to think; throughout this book, we have provided ideas and processes in which the teacher becomes the designer of instruction, and this involves crafting the best learning environment to ensure that all students read, write, speak, listen, and think throughout the schooling process. To continue to become better, we all have areas to improve in our personal lives as well as our professional careers. This takes a commitment to ourselves and becomes even more powerful when that vision and goals are shared with others.

> "Do not claim you want to grow and then run away the minute you feel growing pains."
> ~#BossBabe

As you begin your journey into designing actively engaging lessons that include research-based strategies, remember that although you have the best intentions, some plans may fall flat with students. We encourage you to collaborate with colleagues about your lessons, discussing solutions that make the instruction even better. So many times we try something once, and if it does not give us immediate results (or throws us into the implementation dip), we toss it aside and try something new. By reflecting on our practices and using the ideas of our colleagues, we will be able to persevere through the onslaught of new educational initiatives. When educators start developing common goals and sharing their trials and successes, the profession soars to produce higher achievement for our students.

The comprehension of building curriculum, instruction, and assessment is something that we study in college courses, but as teachers, we must continue to read and connect with other professionals to keep current on best educational practices. In many ways, the changes in communication technology mirror the upkeep that teachers must maintain. For example, consider the telephone: the first devices were on telephone poles, and the user could hear the other people's conversations because the line was shared among multiple families. When the phone made it into individual homes, the user was tied to a cord attached to a unit, and the caller was not identified until one picked up the phone to hear a voice. Voicemail or call-waiting was not available until years later. Even the first cell phones were huge boxes that plugged into the car cigarette lighter, and maybe, they would get reception. If the telephone innovators had not advanced communication devices, people would not be wearing phones on their arms, taking pictures, engaging with friends and family on social media, and playing with other apps, all on the same device into which they talk. Since society is ever-changing, we educators must also continue to learn and grow.

How we learned in our school days may not be the best way to teach the students of today. Curriculum design, assessment creation, and classroom strategy development are all a part of the teaching

"Coming together is a beginning, staying together is progress, and working together is success."
~Henry Ford

Student-Owned Learning: It's more than the teaching; it's about the learning

process and are never finished. We have to keep learning how to make the lessons more interesting for students of today.

Active engagement to motivate students is critical for their learning; in fact, it can be easily compared to playing a musical instrument. When a person first begins to play the instrument, chances are it does not even sound like music. With practice and perseverance, the music becomes tolerable and even enjoyable. The same process is needed as we develop and practice different teaching techniques in the classroom. We have a lot of research that guides us to top practices for student achievement, yet we must be cautious to select the best methods for the needs of the current students in our classrooms. For teachers, we certainly can learn about many different protocols, but it is important to try a few and to master those before tackling others.

The idea of learning from practice is simply to help all students. Differentiation is about building stronger lessons--not necessarily catering to the needs of each individual student. We use the term differentiation when we are making the learning understandable to all of the students in the classroom. Let us use candy to assist with the understanding of differentiation in the classroom: take two packages of M&Ms or Skittles. Pour each package into its own pile on a table. Pretend that the M&Ms/Skittles are two different classrooms in the same grade and/or subject-area.

> "To practice any art, no matter how well or badly, is a way to make your soul grow.
> So do it."
> ~Kurt Vonnegut

Look at the differences between the two "classrooms," and ask yourself:

1. What are some of the differences between the two piles (color, shape, markings, size, etc.)?

2. Which pile is most like your class?

3. How would you design a lesson for this classroom? Would that lesson be different than the one you would design for the other classroom?

4. Are there other ways to think of flexible instructional grouping in these two classrooms?

In applying this concrete image, the take-away is that every classroom contains many different kinds of learners, and we need to design lessons that allow for choice and ultimately, lead to success for ALL of the students.

"Every child has a different learning style and pace. Each child is unique, not only capable of learning but also capable of succeeding."
~Robert John Meehan

If you are like we are as educators, we love to learn new teaching ideas. We have both had the experience, though, of implementing a technique, having it fail the first time, and then abandoning it. On many occasions, we did little reflection on the reason that the method did not work. Wallowing in the implementation dip is not the place where expert teachers reside. Master teachers reflect upon and employ the best methods, sticking with them because they understand that research has shown that they work. Whether we use the direct instruction method or the reciprocal teaching method, we have to be well-versed in different techniques to engage the students. Consider the experience of eating at a restaurant. If you enjoy dining out, you may have visited a buffet in your life. A buffet offers many different choices that at first glance seem pleasing since the eating is

© Debra Kennedy and Angela Smith (2016),
Student-Owned Learning: It's more than the teaching; it's about the learning

immediate and gets right to the heart of the matter: filling the stomach. Though a buffet includes many options, much of the food is of inferior quality. In sit-down restaurants, however, it may take a little longer to order to get exactly what you want; in most cases, though, the outcome is far superior. As in a sit-down restaurant, teachers need to offer choices to students while balancing the quality of those options. Doing a variety of "stuff" can turn into busy work rather than actual student-owned learning. Time spent in planning an activity and considering it from all angles will save time and minimize the intervention after the lesson.

The concentration of most teacher evaluation systems is in two parts of the lesson: planning and delivery. When reviewing the items rated by the evaluation, most point to the planning of the lesson. When observing teachers, we have heard them bemoan the lack of time for planning; unfortunately, many simply do not work through the planning phase as much as they should. It seems, though, that time is one of those factors often blamed for an inadequate product, whether talking about cleaning the house, washing the car, or practicing a new skill. We know that we all have twenty-four hours in a day and sixty minutes in an hour, and no matter how we use those minutes, we still only have sixty minutes. We teachers must ask ourselves: "what do I do with the minutes that I have each hour?" The goal setting discussed in the last chapter is also applicable to adults. In your life, you need to decide where your passions are priority, and then give the time to what you hold most dear. If you are striving to help students achieve in their lives, then time must be spent planning for this event to occur.

> "24 hours, just like everybody else. There is nobody who created and go 25, and there is nobody who cheated and gave you 23. No excuses."
> ~#BossBabe

You then spend the time above and beyond the contracted day to be the best that you can be in your profession.

> "Always bear in mind that your own resolution to succeed is more important than any other one thing."
> ~Abraham Lincoln

Passion is what makes us go places that we never dreamed we could go in our lifetime. Writing this book and sharing our dreams of what good teaching should look and sound like has been our passion that we continue to pass onto people reading this book. Meeting teachers and presenting this material in an easy to understand format is still part of our personal goals. We both have families, work in schools on a regular basis, and are involved in community events, yet we schedule time together on a regular basis to keep each other growing and learning while contributing to the educational community.

To conclude, we leave you with one last thought: What are your action steps to continue to learn and grow? To be a great teacher, you can never stop learning. Never stop learning; never stop growing!

STUDENT-OWNED LEARNING
APPENDIX
SOME EXTRA RESOURCES

Books for literacy strategies

Burke, J. (2009) *Content Area Reading*. New York, NY:
        Scholastic.
Daniels, H. & Steineke, N. (2011) *Texts and Lessons for Content-
        Area Reading*. Portsmouth, NH: Heinemann.
Hayes Jacobs, H. (2006) *Active Literacy Across the Curriculum*.
        Parrsipany, NJ: Eye on Education.

CHAPTER THREE: DIFFERENTIATION RESOURCES

Differentiation Techniques from A-Z : Here are differentiation

protocols with definitions and websites.

	Differentiation Protocol	Definition	Website Resource
A	Anchor activities	ongoing self-directed activities that relate to a major concept of the content	http://www.rec4.com/filestore/rec4_anchoractivitypacket_080513.pdf
B	Benchmarks	students track their own progress for meeting the standard	http://thegridmethod.com/about
C	Cubing	students toss a cube and complete the activity or question that is on the top face	http://www.readwritethink.org/classroom-resources/student-interactives/mystery-cube-30059.html
D	Different modalities	teacher represents concepts kinesthetically, visually, and auditorily	https://msdillard.wordpress.com/2013/01/05/the-four-modalities-of-learning/
E	Entrance/Exit tickets	students write what they know; what they did for homework; what confuses them, etc.	http://www.gooru.org/
F	Flexible grouping	cooperative project groups arranged by interests, ability, similarities, tasks, etc.	http://www.adprima.com/grouping.htm

	Differentiation Protocol	Definition	Website Resource
G	Group investigations	students are grouped by interest and decide what to study	https://www.youtube.com/watch?v=iBplYaL95mg
H	Homework	students craft their own homework assignments	http://www.educationworld.com/a_curr/curr373.shtml
I	Independent study	students plan and execute their own projects	http://www.itm-info.com/wildfire/images/activities.pdf
J	Journaling	students reflect on learning or select a journal prompt from a menu of choices	http://www.dailyteachingtools.com/journal-writing-prompts.html
K	Knowledge visualization	students create their own pictures of vocabulary or concepts to make it more meaningful	http://www.scholastic.com/teachers/lesson-plan/activity-plan-mixed-ages-make-picture-dictionary
L	Learning contracts	student and teacher agree a method that allows for exploration of a certain content	https://wsddifferentiation.wikispaces.com/file/view/Learning+Contract.pdf
M	Menus	students select their assignment from a list of choices set up as a restaurant menu or tic tac toe board	http://www.readwritethink.org/files/resources/lesson_images/lesson842/VM0104Menu.pdf
N	Note-taking	students learn different strategies for note taking based on their favored modality for learning	http://universitycollege.illinoisstate.edu/downloads/Different%20Learning%20Styles.pdf
O	Organizing portfolios	students complete several assignments on a topic and select which to submit for evaluation	https://www.teachervision.com/assessment/teaching-methods/20153.html
P	Problem-based learning	students learn through solving an open-ended problem	http://www.studygs.net/pbl.htm
Q	Questions	teacher uses critical thinking questions, or students write their own review questions	http://beyondpenguins.ehe.osu.edu/issue/energy-and-the-polar-environment/questioning-techniques-research-based-strategies-for-teachers

	Differentiation Protocol	Definition	Website Resource
R	Resident expert	students become an expert on content and then share with their team	http://www.nsrfharmony.org/ system/files/protocols/jigsaw_0 .pdf
S	Stations	centers are set up in a classroom, and few students complete different activities at each	https://www.teachervision.com/ learning-center/new-teacher/48462.html
T	Tiered lessons	students work on activities designed for their ability or interest	https://daretodifferentiate. wikispaces.com/Tiering/
U	Using color coding	students identify parts of a problem or essay, denoting it with certain colors	http://www.facultyware.uconn. edu/products/16/McCormac Condon_Gentile.pdf

CHAPTER FOUR: DIRECT INSTRUCTION AND RECIPROCAL TEACHING RESOURCES

Concept Maps

David Hyerle: *Visual Tools for Thinking Maps*: a website with

extensive explanations and examples of concept maps.

Resource: http://dft.designsforthinking.com/?page_id=15

A Visual Example of Reciprocal Teaching

Reciprocal teaching visual example:

https://www.youtube.com/watch?v=8oXskcnb4RA

Question Stems

- https://tpri.wikispaces.com/file/view/05-2Bloom-16-17+Stems+for+Instruction.pdf
- http://svesd.net/files/DOK_Question_Stems.pdf

Deb
prolearningcurve@ gmail. com

43790757R00076

Made in the USA
San Bernardino, CA
28 December 2016